HOW TO DRAW
AND PAINT
SUCCESSFULLY

HOW TO DRAW AND PAINT SUCCESSFULLY

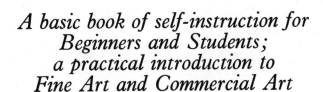

*A basic book of self-instruction for
Beginners and Students;
a practical introduction to
Fine Art and Commercial Art*

by
H. A. BOX
and
T. R. DIPPLE, M.I.P.A.

A. THOMAS & CO
PRESTON

"REPRINTED NOVEMBER 1963"
Printed in Great Britain by
Charles Birchall & Sons Limited
Liverpool & London
"SECOND EDITION PRINTED 1966"

CONTENTS

PREFACE

This book is in the following four parts: 1. Learning to Draw; 2. Painting in Water-colours; 3. Painting in Oils; and 4. Commercial Art. It is therefore a general book for the beginner and for the student, for the many people who have no grandiose ideas of their capabilities as artists but who from time to time think about drawing and painting, for older people who would like to try but who are unsure of how to set about it, and for younger people who are ready to tackle anything at all. For the student who wishes to follow an art career, this book offers both a foundation on which he can build as well as an introduction to the different lines of development which are open to him.

Drawing is not difficult and it is a natural form of self-expression. Some are content to copy exactly what they see, others prefer to interpret. Today, particularly, abstraction and graphic design has a strong appeal, influenced by contemporary trends in printed literature, product manufacture, architecture and space missile exploration. We are all partially influenced by these things in our approach to drawing and painting. We take stock of what is around us. And we see that the old buildings are still there, the colour and design of nature remains the same irrespective of what we think or do, so that we can't help looking both backward and forward at the artistic possibilities that will always exist.

This book, in a very straight-forward way, can help you to overcome the initial problems in drawing and painting. It is a starting point for you. After teaching the basic principles of drawing, it then introduces you to the many facets of drawing and painting, both for pleasure and as a profitable career. The materials that artists use for various kinds of work are described in each case, so that you will know what materials to buy and how best to use them.

The wide field of 'commercial art' offers many opportunities of profitable employment. Practical instruction for students and beginners in the art of 'drawing and reproduction' is given in part 4; and even those who wish to draw and paint solely for pleasure can profit from a study of commercial art methods.

Anyone can draw. Anyone, that is, who is prepared to learn the basic rules of procedure. The proficiency that you attain depends on the amount of time that you give to practice and the degree of effort that you put into it. Above all, *enjoy* your drawing and painting.

Whatever may be your aim as an artist, this many-sided introduction to drawing and painting can start you on your way.

PART ONE

LEARNING TO DRAW

GETTING USED TO DRAWING

Before we proceed in detail to composition, perspective, figure-drawing and so on, get to practical grips with drawing right away. An interesting and instructive way to start, and to help find out how good or bad you are at this stage, is by sketching simple-shaped objects. Never draw from flat copies; always from real, solid things. Confine yourself to simple objects in the home, sketching wherever you have moments to spare. Now, what are the minimum materials you need and how do you begin?

First, you buy from a local printer 50 sheets of Bank paper, size 21 in. × 16 in. This paper is cheap and good enough for your purpose. Next, you require HB and 2B pencils. The HB lead pencil is one part clay and nine parts graphite. Softer and blacker leads are produced when the graphite is increased and we get B, 2B, 3B and so on; a harder lead results when the proportion of clay is increased, such as F (firm), H, 2H and so on. Sharpen your pencil at the opposite end to the letters indicating the type; a smooth, well-tapered cut. You will need a soft India rubber, and if you do not possess a drawing board a thick sheet of hardboard or plywood will serve for the time being.

You may decide later to do most of your sketching standing as this gives greater freedom of arm movement, but to begin you will find it better to sit. Your board should be in a sloping position, and holding your pencil with four fingers underneath and thumb on top provides an easier movement.

Start by sketching in outline only. Try to get clean, sharp lines and use your eraser as little as possible. As you draw your objects keep a careful watch on your proportions in depth and width.

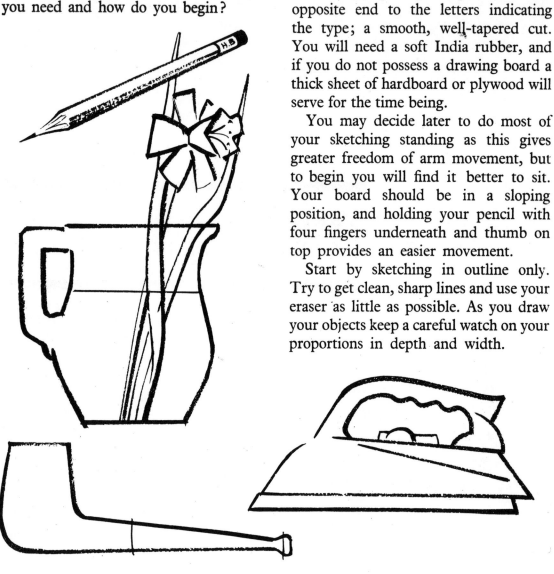

8

LIGHT AND SHADE

As you become more accurate and confident you should begin to introduce shading until you get depth and form and a three-dimensional appearance. The sphere is a simple shape with which to start and you can progress to more interesting and complicated objects such as a wine bottle, china or pot ornament, cooking utensils, and toys. You will find plenty of subject material in the house and tool shed.

The globe above looks to have depth because of the reflected light on the shadow side.

As you draw your objects observe carefully the light and dark parts, also gradual changes from light to dark, and show this in your drawings. Light and shade is effected by the direction of the light and by the nature of the objects themselves. Now, outline and shading are used together, and your outlining will become less rigid. Extremes of light and shade, in-between half-tones, and cast shadows are all used. Re-arrange your objects to get different light and shade effects. Study your object carefully from this aspect before you start to draw so that you have a clear idea in your mind of the effect which you wish to achieve. Never add shading aimlessly. Every line, every tone, should be deliberate and meaningful.

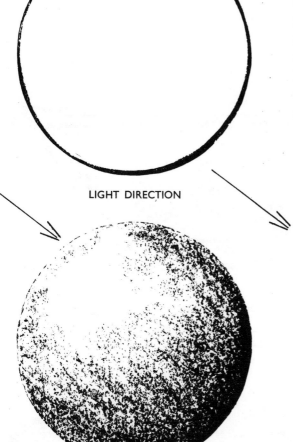

LIGHT DIRECTION

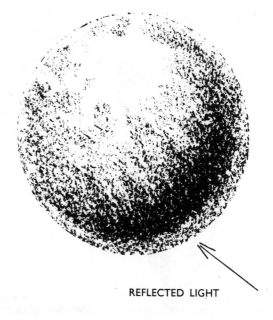

REFLECTED LIGHT

9

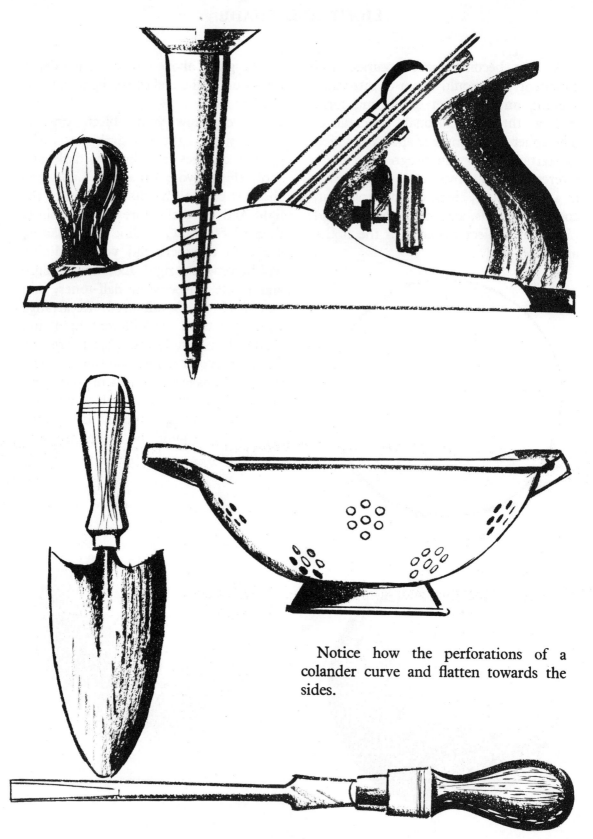

Notice how the perforations of a colander curve and flatten towards the sides.

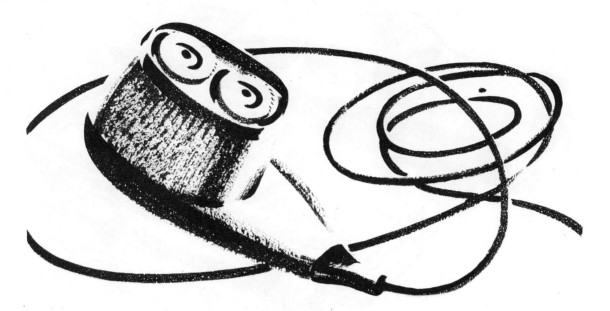

Now we try an exercise without using any outline. You can draw your frame lines very lightly using your H pencil, and build up from these, but you rely entirely on shading to give shape, dimension and depth.

Two parked cars show how the shadow side of one vehicle can outline for you the contour shape of the other.

The purpose of drawing in this way is to introduce you to painting. Try to think in terms of areas rather than perimeter lines. Very few things in this world consist of lines alone. Drawing is a kind of modelling and in this manner you aim to express depth and form.

Here we make full use of both outline and shading, including medium-tones, in order to convey texture. This is to say, we make the material of the subject recognizable by its surface appearance as well as by its shape.

Very often, the use of outline is a matter for your own discretion and depends on the effect which you wish to convey. Use outline where necessary to give sharpness to your drawing. Use it to accentuate depth and fullness of shape, to give texture, perhaps to add strength and dramatic effect.

The extra pencil used in this sketch is the 4B carpenter's pencil with a rectangular lead. It is useful in quick sketching where action is taking place and time is limited. You may find it easier to break off and use about ½ inch of lead as the whole pencil is rather unwieldy.

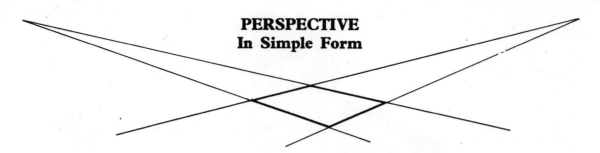

PERSPECTIVE
In Simple Form

Before you decide to close the book at this point we hasten to assure you that the subject of perspective is probably not as difficult as you may suppose. What is perspective? It is the relation of size and distance. The subject can be approached in a simple way and this is done on pages 16 to 22. Let us proceed step-by-step in a simple form, starting with the horizon line.

therefore converge downwards and the road and pavement lines converge upwards. These lines all converge at the same point on the horizon because they are parallel to each other. The effect is three dimensional and without adding any more detail we have achieved an impression of distance on a flat surface. Note the gate on the left. This is not parallel to the roadway and its perspec-

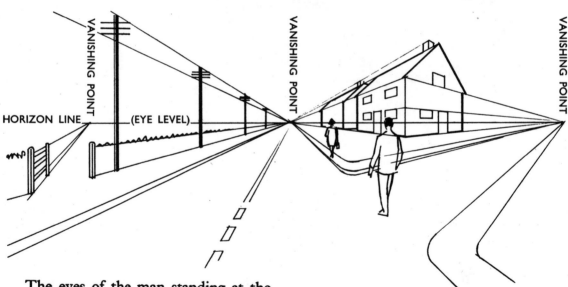

The eyes of the man standing at the roadside are directed at a point where the road disappears from sight (marked with a dot). His eyes may be turned to the left or right but they remain on the horizon line, the level of his eyes. Now, all lines below the horizon line recede upwards to it, all lines above the horizon recede downwards to it. The roof lines of the houses and the telephone wires

tive lines therefore have a different converging point on the horizon; all its parallel lines converge upwards to meet at one point on the horizon. The road branching to the right is a similar example; the top and bottom lines of the end house wall also converge on the horizon at this point, with all the intervening lines of bricks if they were shown.

We will now take a simple object and draw it in perspective when there is no convenient horizon line available. The object may be above the eye level, below it, or across it. The thing to remember is that all parallel lines of the object meet at one point on the eye level, either to the left or right.

The first brick is shown below eye level; its parallel lines converge upwards to the eye level line. The centre illustration shows the brick above eye level with its parallel sides converging downwards and these meet at left and right on the eye level line. The third position shows the brick drawn level with the eye; lines above eye level converge downwards to meet on the eye line, with lines parallel to these running upwards from below eye level.

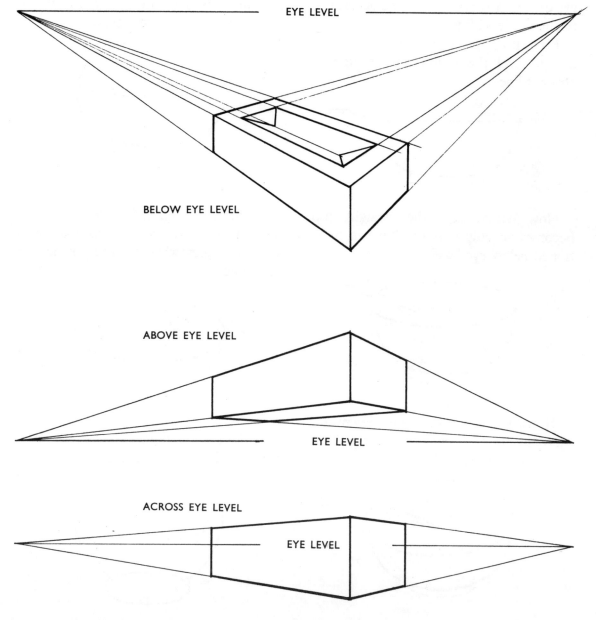

EYE LEVEL

BELOW EYE LEVEL

ABOVE EYE LEVEL

EYE LEVEL

ACROSS EYE LEVEL

EYE LEVEL

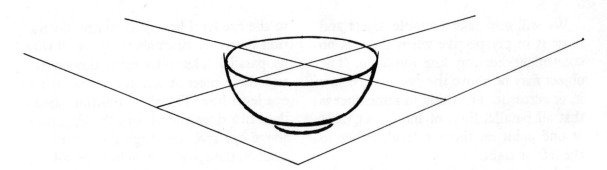

Our next step in simple perspective shows what happens when circular objects are drawn in varying positions according to the eye level line.

First, if the top of the bowl is exactly at eye level the round top becomes a straight line.

Now notice how the straight top becomes an ellipse as the bowl is positioned below eye level.

If we take an even more downward view the ellipse becomes deeper and the sides narrower (foreshortened).

Looking almost directly down on the bowl, the top is very nearly a full circle and the sides have foreshortened so much that they are only just visible.

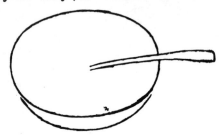

To draw an ellipse, first draw the axis, then the axle. Always draw axle and axis at right angles whatever the position of the subject.

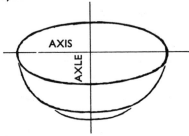

If the bowl is higher than the level of your eye it will look like this.

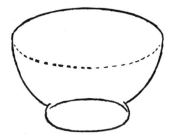

Now let us combine our two shapes, circles and rectangles or squares. First, we draw an horizon or eye level line. All objects parallel with each other have same vanishing points. 1, 2, 3 and 4 all have parallel sides and all are parallel with each other, so they have the same vanishing points whatever their size or position in the picture. No. 5 is parallel with all these but our position is between (see sketch, page 15), so lines running away from us will meet on the right. Object 6 is not parallel with anything and has its own vanishing points. Note that the tubes 7 and 8 are parallel with each other, also both same length.

Object 9 shows how an ellipse flattens as it nears eye level; 10 and 11 show ellipses at an angle. To draw these correctly always construct the axle at right angles to the axis.

The chimney rises above eye level; notice how the ellipses are flat at eye level, deepening as they move away from it. The chimney appears to narrow as it rises; perpendicular lines converge slightly as they move upwards or downwards away from eye level. In this way the impression of height or depth is given, see downward view of cigarette.

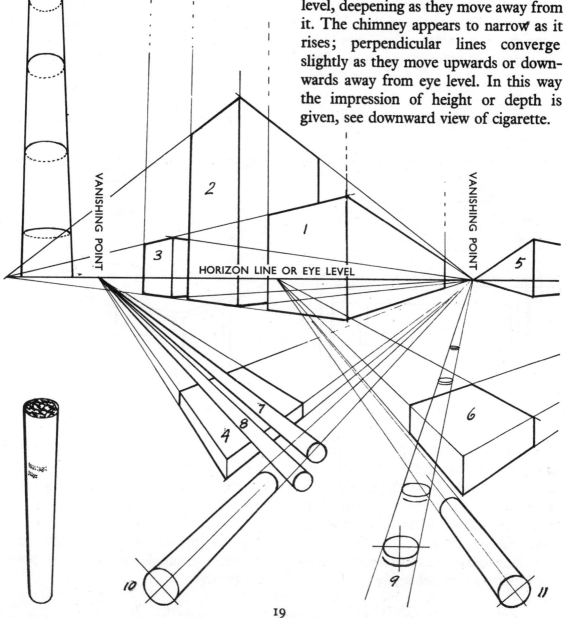

VANISHING POINT

VANISHING POINT

HORIZON LINE OR EYE LEVEL

Simple Exercises

Draw your horizon or eye level line first. If your drawing is imaginary this line can be anywhere across the paper you choose; the higher the eye line the more downward will be your view of the object you draw, the lower the eye line the more upward your view.

On this page a 'box' shape is shown in the forms of a book and a table, below eye level. In the first illustration they are drawn face view in one-point perspective; the second illustration shows an angle view, two front sides visible, the most you could see at once, using two-point perspective in the same way.

Note. Your vanishing points will not always appear actually on the eye line which you draw across your paper. Sometimes your perspective lines slope up or down very little, according to your view of the object, and you would need an enormous sheet of paper to draw your eye line long enough to reach a particular vanishing point. Where it is necessary, imagine your eye line extending much wider than the paper and estimate the direction of any parallel lines which would meet on it beyond the paper.

ONE-POINT PERSPECTIVE, FACE VIEW

TWO-POINT PERSPECTIVE, ANGLE VIEW

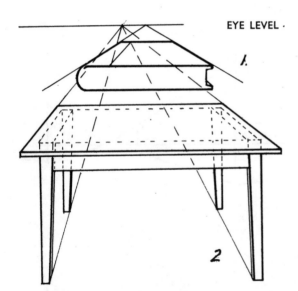

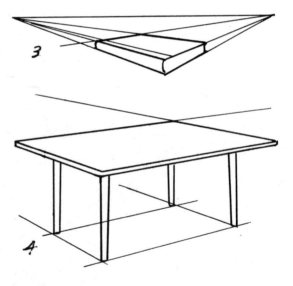

EYE LEVEL ·

1. Place a box (or thick book, upright, not flat as shown here, so that you have a shape view which is different from our example), on the table exactly in front of you and draw it in one-point perspective below eye level.

2. Now draw the table itself, in one-point perspective, below eye level.

3. Turn it sideways so that you see two sides and draw it in two-point perspective.

4. Sit opposite one corner, and draw the table in simple outline in two-point perspective.

20

For practice in simple perspective, draw any objects that are rectangular or tubular in shape. Remember the main rule: all parallel lines of an object converge upwards or downwards to the eye level line, and would eventually meet at a point along it, to the right or left. The exception to this rule is when you stand immediately in front of an object so that lines run parallel with eye level or horizon: an example of this is the table on page 20, directly in front of the artist. (If these lines were extended sufficiently, those running to the left would converge upward to meet at one point on the eye line, similarly with lines extended to the right, but immediately in front of the artist they appear parallel with the eye line). Notice the deeper ellipse of the paint-pot compared with the bucket to indicate a more downward view. Draw your perspective lines roughly, more or less guessing them once you know the simple rules, and you will very quickly acquire the habit of drawing your objects instinctively in correct perspective. In free hand drawing you should now begin to 'visualize' eye line and lines which vanish to the horizon, drawing a few essential guide lines to help you.

EYE LEVEL

Taking some of the objects shown on the preceding page we build a composition study in order to practise the relation of large objects to small in perspective. We see that the tin in the foreground has slight or 'slow' perspective, whilst the perspective of the house is more apparent. This is because the side of the house in view is larger than the tin, in its dimensions. The smaller the object, the less obvious is the perspective. The matchbox shown beside the tin has hardly any apparent perspective, but still the outline shape converges to a point on the eye level or horizon line.

PERSPECTIVE
A More Advanced Study

When a large object such as a building with windows and doors, is being drawn in perspective, it becomes essential to locate the exact position of the centre of the building, in perspective. This is necessary so that windows, for example, can be shown in their correct position and proportion. To arrive at this central point draw two diagonals, A and B. The centre of the building is the point where these bisect each other. As you can see, by bisecting each half again, a further division is made.

If you divide the back line of the floor into equal parts, and the front line of the floor into the same number of equal parts, this is the first stage in achieving the effect of a chequered pattern floor. The diagonal dotted lines bisect the floor in the same way as those on the wall of the building, to give the positions of the crossing lines.

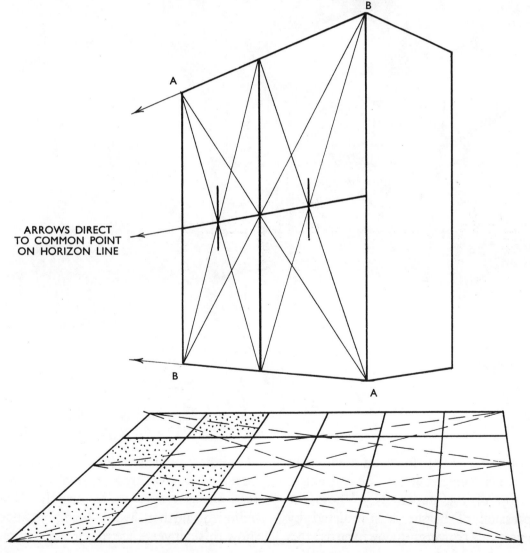

ARROWS DIRECT
TO COMMON POINT
ON HORIZON LINE

You are looking down on a city and you can visualize your eye line way above the top of the paper. Note how the impression of height is stimulated by the verticals converging downwards; this impression of height (or depth) can be increased as required by making your verticals converge more acutely. The buildings farther away, being smaller, show this convergence to a lesser degree.

PERSPECTIVE CONSTRUCTION

This example shows the use of rectangular shapes and ellipses as in drawing a car.

Notice that the diagonal lines cross at a point which is the centre in perspective of the rectangular shape.

Draw in the axle lines, then add a wheel to the frame. The axis is always at right angles to the axle.

Remember that all parallel lines should converge slightly as they would eventually meet at their vanishing points, one for the lines running upward to the left and one for those running upward to the right, on a common horizon line.

By building up to a long box shape (dotted lines) you can now draw in the actual body shape and wheels in more detail.

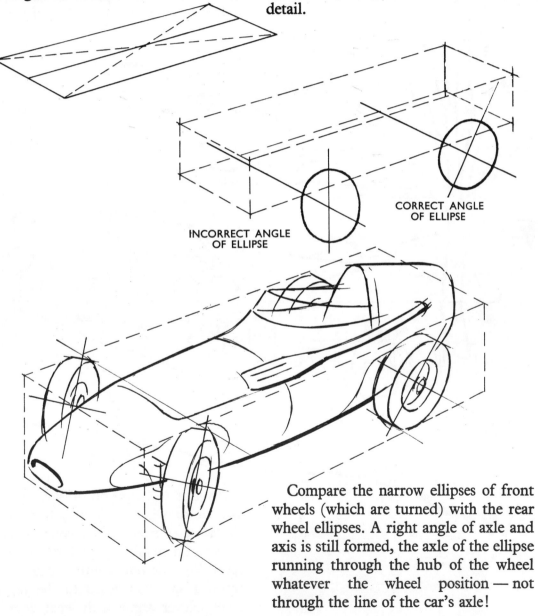

CORRECT ANGLE OF ELLIPSE

INCORRECT ANGLE OF ELLIPSE

Compare the narrow ellipses of front wheels (which are turned) with the rear wheel ellipses. A right angle of axle and axis is still formed, the axle of the ellipse running through the hub of the wheel whatever the wheel position — not through the line of the car's axle!

Let us take a simple landscape scene. Perspective creeps in to affect the clouds, trees, houses and even the ground. This emphasizes the need for you to understand at least the rudiments of perspective. The chief difficulty met with in keeping perspective accurate in landscapes arises from the lack of straight line rectangular shapes.

Establish your horizon, then draw in those parts that appear immediately above and below the horizon, such as hills, trees and buildings. This will establish the angle and perspective of the main parts. Now sketch in the lower half of the scene, keeping the same perspective. Remember that when sketching your sky, the farther away the cloud shapes the slimmer they become, until they are almost a line as they near the horizon.

Of course, it is practice that will do most to increase your skill and here are

a few tips to help you on your way. If you are drawing or painting from something, or someone, hold your pencil or brush horizontal at your horizon or eye level. You can now see the definite slope upward and downward to the horizon level. Never argue with what your eye sees. Whatever you see, and however you see it, draw it that way. You are training your vision equally as much as your hand, learning to draw what the eye sees and not what the mind knows to be there. The appearance of an object will vary according to its distance from you, the angle of vision and in its relation to surrounding objects.

With very tall subjects such as, for instance, skyscraper buildings, avoid exaggeration in perspective or you will produce an effect similar to that obtained by the camera with its one eye. Strictly speaking, as you raise your head and gaze upward you have a higher horizon line than the true one, therefore you

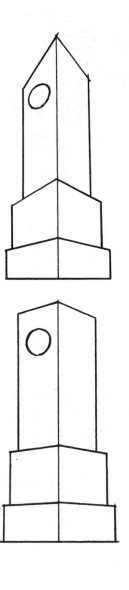

should reduce the sharp angles as shown here. The second example looks much better and is less like a photograph. Never copy direct from a photograph; you should only refer to photographs for intricate detail.

All the information given here is to help your pictures to look right and this is all that we are trying to achieve.

Exaggerated perspective is another thing altogether when a special or unusual effect is desired. We have mentioned in previous pages how very acute perspective lines can be used to give the impression of great height or distance, and this is something worth experimenting with when you have mastered normal per-spective.

Here are two exercises, one outdoors and the other indoors. If you succeed in doing a reasonable drawing of each without reference to the previous pages you should feel well satisfied. If you are able to stand in a position to observe a straight stretch of railway you will be given a good object lesson in perspective. You will see the tracks, although parallel, converge toward the horizon. If you watch a train approaching or moving away from you, the carriages will appear progressively shorter although each is the same length; this is foreshortening.

In the top sketch you will see that the eye level line is about one-fifth of the way from the bottom; the parallel lines of the train would converge at a point in the margin of the page on the left. In the bottom sketch, the eye level line is visualized just above the top of where the illustration finishes.

Perspective and composition go hand-in-hand. It is necessary to be able to apply perspective naturally and easily before we proceed to the next stage, which is composition.

Composition is the art of arranging the parts of your picture so that they form an organized whole. There is no single formula for good composition but to help you to have this ability, that is the ability to compose your picture so that it has unity and balance, an acquaintance with certain basic geometric forms and the relation these have to good composition, will help you considerably.

These basic patterns must not be regarded too rigidly, and they can be varied, or combined, as your sense of composition develops.

But before proceeding to these basic forms let us take note of some faults to be avoided. Also, illustrations for magazines have often to be fitted to confined and awkward-shaped spaces, necessitating a different approach.

Top left. FAULTS. House too big for picture. Not enough of tree at left to give it shape. Lamp-post coincides with the line of the house and competes with it. Similarly, top of tree above the roof is misleading. End of house is exactly at

edge of picture. Fence 'chopped in half' seems to be falling out of picture. Distance view is too confined.

Bottom left. FAULTS. House too small, placed dead centre of picture, road occupies too much space and drops out of picture centrally. Trees too equal in size, too evenly placed. Background hill rises and falls from unseen point behind the house. Nowhere for eye to settle happily.

Top right. IMPROVED COMPOSITION. Notice the way in which the faults in the other two compositions have been corrected here. The figures add extra interest to this picture.

A small object which is very dark can be as prominent, or more so, than a pale coloured object which is several times larger. So that in composition the balance of light and dark is as important as placing, and both must be considered together. Positioning the parts of a picture is important in itself, but a good arrangement can look 'out of plumb' if an excess of dark or light in one area is allowed to drag everything to one side.

Some faults are painfully obvious, at other times the cause of what is wrong is not so easy to discern. Here is one simple and practical guide. Divide a rectangle representing the extremities of your picture, into thirds. Then decide what is to be the centre or point of interest in your picture and place it at any point where the dotted lines bisect.

Start with simple basic shapes, such as the triangle and the rectangle. Many variations of this theme are possible; some ideas are shown on this page and you can develop ideas of your own.

SIMPLE STUDIES IN PLACING AND BALANCE

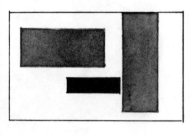

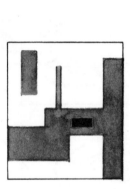

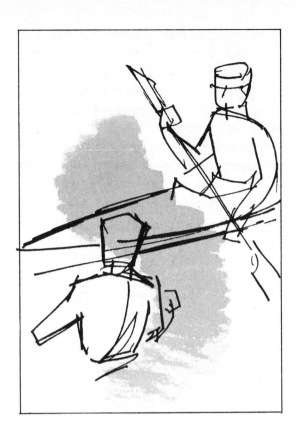

BUILDING UP COMPOSITION

IN STAGES

Sketch in quite roughly the position of action, or point of interest, then fill in other details to build up the scene, bearing in mind the tone values in relation to size. At the same time remember to keep your perspective and proportion as accurate as possible. Avoid large dark areas unless the whole picture is deliberately deep-toned. Make as much use as possible of white space and light tones against dark.

COMPOSITION

SUMMARY

A picture should look complete without a frame and hold the viewer's interest without any tendency for the eye to wander off to the edge. Shapes or areas of colour help to give solidity. Sweeping curves suggest movement and a feeling of space.

Be wary of attempting to show too much detail. Ensure that the emphasis, area or point of interest, lies well into the picture. Do not have too many things happening in one picture; it is generally the best thing to simplify the subject as much as possible. Aim to get the important parts of your sketch pointing inwards, and overlapping or joining. In this way you will show a complete and integrated scene and avoid an impression of an arrangement of disconnected parts.

Our last example of composition (below) is an arrangement without an actual point of interest, yet everything in the picture appears to circle towards the space to the right of the well. This example is meant to show that the basic rules of good composition, like the basic rules of most things, are capable of varied interpretation. But you will never get a good composition without consciously arranging it, generally working outwards from your centre of interest to the edges of your picture.

The basic instruction given in this section can enable you to draw human figures that are correctly proportioned and in the pose or action that you wish to portray. For this purpose some knowledge of anatomy and skeleton construction is necessary.

You should draw from life whenever you have the opportunity (more about this difficulty in a moment), and this is much easier when you possess the simple bone and muscle-form knowledge of the human figure. This book will give you that knowledge. Then you can practice by copying and memorizing illustrations from this book, studying the work of good artists, and by constant observation and using imagination you can develop your creative figure drawing ability. Now, before we proceed further, let us deal with this problem of opportunity to draw from the live model.

If you were asked what is the chief stumbling block in nude figure drawing for the learner who is unable to attend art school life classes, the answer would be that of persuading someone to pose for you and having a suitable room in which to work. Even your best friend will shy at posing in the nude. This book, let us assume, is for those who do not attend art school, so how do we overcome this problem? This is what we suggest to you. Go to places where you will see people who are only partially clothed, to outdoor swimming pools, and beaches, for example. Here, you will be able to sketch from life people of all ages, shapes and sizes. The female figure is less exposed than the male, of course,

but even so you will increase your knowledge and ability considerably by such practice.

Another useful aid is the mirror. This is especially useful for sketching hands, arms, legs and feet in a variety of positions. This method has its limitations, and it is difficult to draw a rear view of oneself without a complicated arrangement of mirrors, but it remains a most useful aid.

After you have learned how to draw the nude figure you can then draw the clothed figure. In the following studies we have sometimes shown the one above the other, and this is to illustrate some of the points which you should keep in mind when drawing the clothed figure and which we will briefly explain here.

The drapery is important. The pose of the body inside the clothes does affect their appearance, sometimes considerably. But to show a woman in a formal or slightly relaxed pose and wearing a dress tailored to her figure may mean simply superimposing the dress on to a drawing of the nude, whereas clothes on a man in a similar pose may follow lines very different to the nude figure. A man's clothes generally hang more loosely and may mould to the figure only at points of stress according to the pose. In some of the following illustrations the same figure is shown nude and clothed to illustrate these differences.

Fashion drawings of men and women used in advertising art emphasize certain features of the figure. This kind of figure drawing is referred to on page 111.

FIGURE PROPORTION

When we say that the length of the human figure is $7\frac{1}{2}$ times the length of the head this is of course a generalization. But this proportion represents the average figure and on this page we are going to state the simple rules of proportion, and illustrate them, so that you can memorize them and apply them in practice.

The head measurement is from the crown to the chin; the second 'head measurement' is from chin to the nipples of the breast; third, from here to the navel; fourth is from navel to the top of the legs; fifth, sixth and seventh extend from here to the ankle with the knee coming in the centre of the sixth; and the final $\frac{1}{2}$ head measurement is from ankle to the sole of the foot.

When the two arms are extended horizontally, the distance between the tips of the second fingers of each hand equals the height of the figure. The width of the shoulders equals 2 heads in the male figure, less in the female figure.

Conceive your figure as a whole; do not draw in the parts until you have proportioned the complete figure. Later, when drawing figures in varying poses, visualize the figure as having three basic masses—head, chest and pelvic region, which can be joined together in varying ways. The three parts comprising each arm and leg can also each be connected in varying positions. With more advanced practice, and more striking or difficult poses, remember the laws of perspective, including foreshortening. Exercises on page 55 illustrate figures in perspective.

A plumb line is useful for checking the angles and pose of the figure (see page 43).

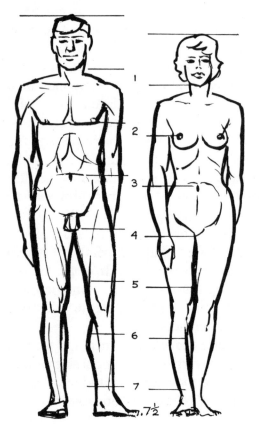

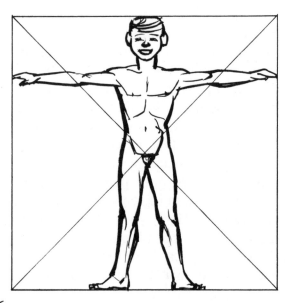

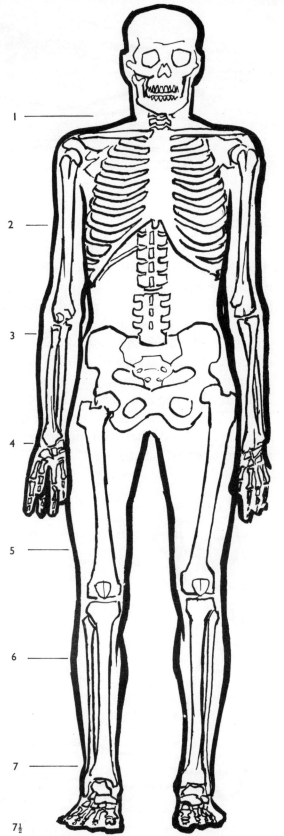

SIMPLE BUILD-UP OF THE FIGURE

You should start by dividing the human figure into simple block shapes in order to become acquainted with proportion, pose and perspective. These basic shapes are explained on page 42. You will find that it will help you if you practise sketching in the whole figure in this manner first, adding true form and detail afterwards.

1

2

3

4

5

6

7

7½

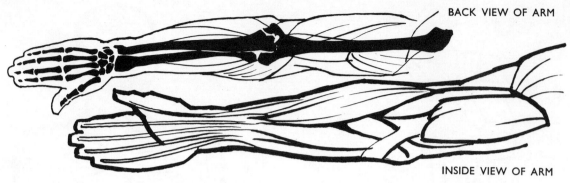

BACK VIEW OF ARM

INSIDE VIEW OF ARM

FRONT AND REAR VIEW
OF LEGS

THE ARM

As with the figure itself, remember that the arm is a continuous limb and not three disjointed parts—upper arm, forearm, hand. In whatever position these three parts may be individually, they remain interrelated, the pose of one part affecting the appearance of another, and the pose of the forearm may alter the look of the shoulder. Any triangular shapes formed between the arm and the body are a good check on proportion; see the example on page 44.

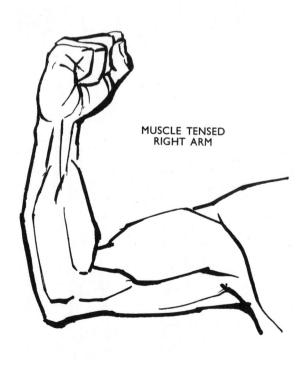

MUSCLE TENSED
RIGHT ARM

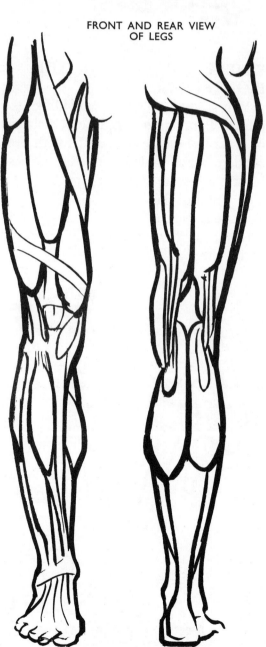

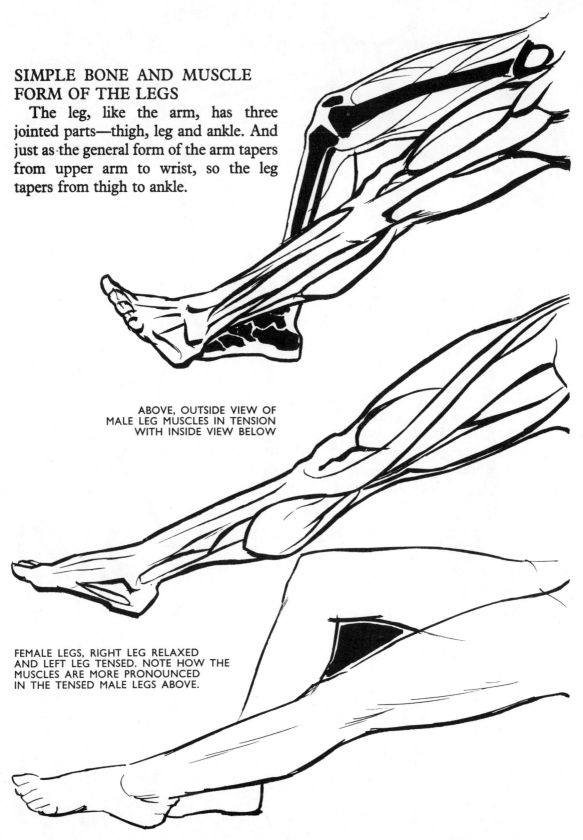

SIMPLE BONE AND MUSCLE FORM OF THE LEGS

The leg, like the arm, has three jointed parts—thigh, leg and ankle. And just as the general form of the arm tapers from upper arm to wrist, so the leg tapers from thigh to ankle.

ABOVE, OUTSIDE VIEW OF MALE LEG MUSCLES IN TENSION WITH INSIDE VIEW BELOW

FEMALE LEGS, RIGHT LEG RELAXED AND LEFT LEG TENSED. NOTE HOW THE MUSCLES ARE MORE PRONOUNCED IN THE TENSED MALE LEGS ABOVE.

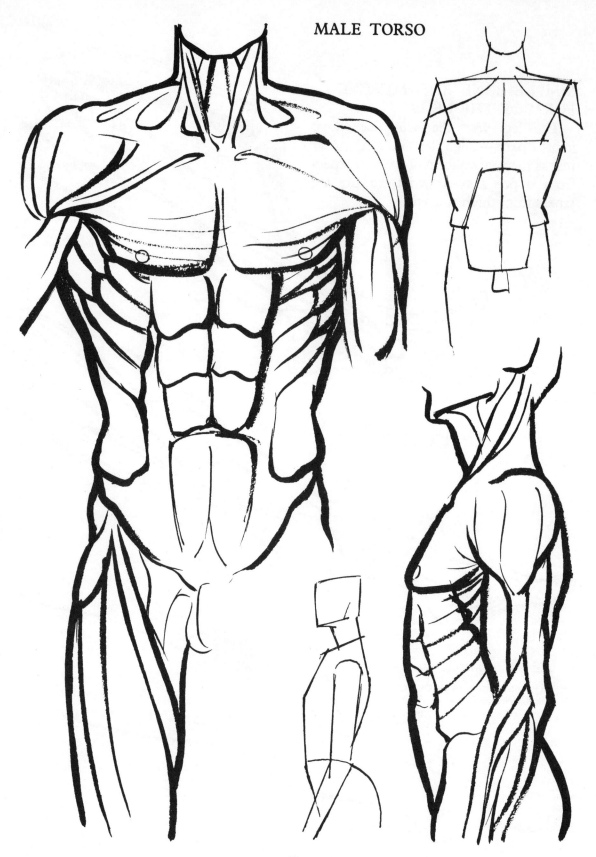

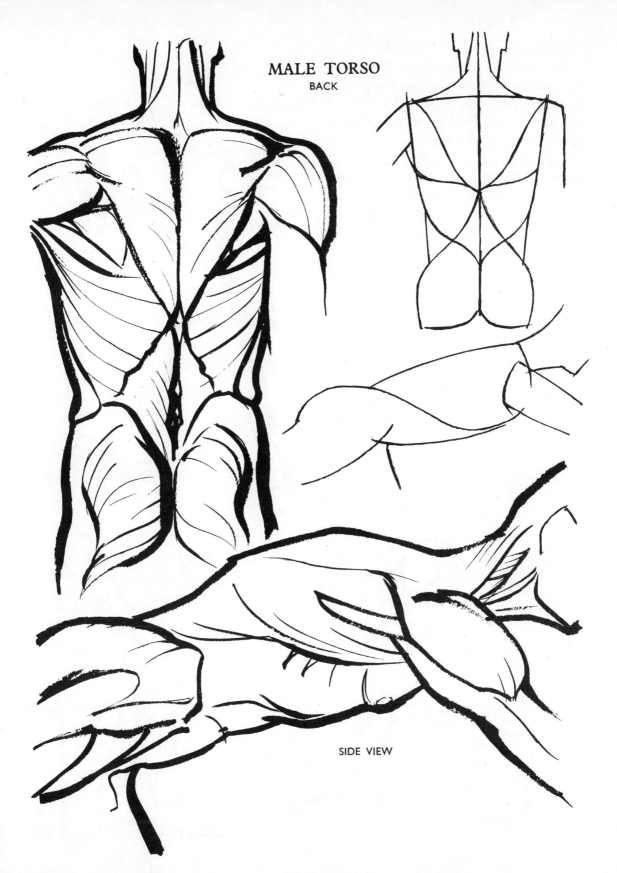

MALE TORSO
BACK

SIDE VIEW

41

PLANNING YOUR FIGURE

Your first figure drawings should use three simple concepts such as those in the figures on page 37. These are a cube for the head, a slightly tapering rectangle for the chest, and a square for the hips. These three basic parts can be in various positions. Attached to them are the neck, arms and legs which can turn and twist in their constituent parts. When drawing these shapes, remember your perspective rules. On this page we have progressed a stage further in building up our figure form.

MALE FIGURES

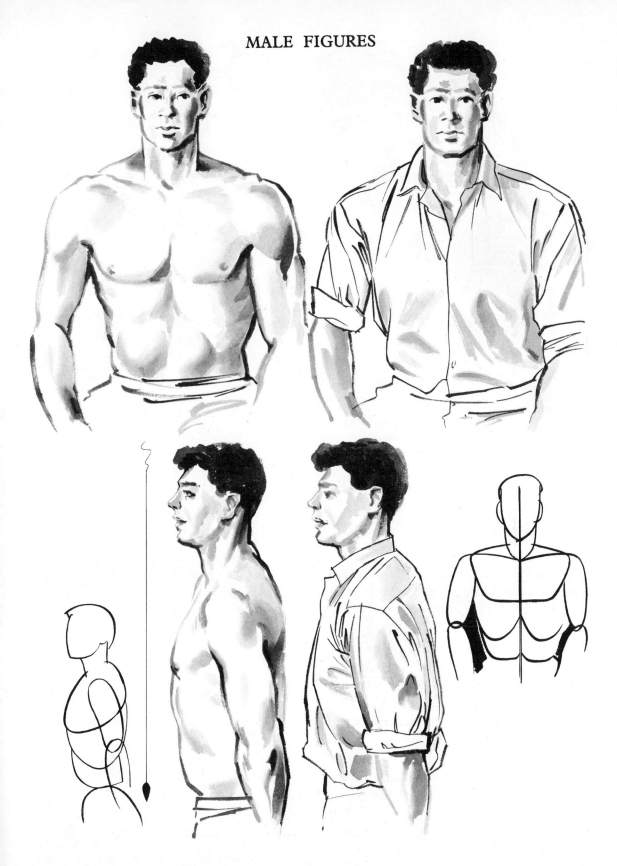

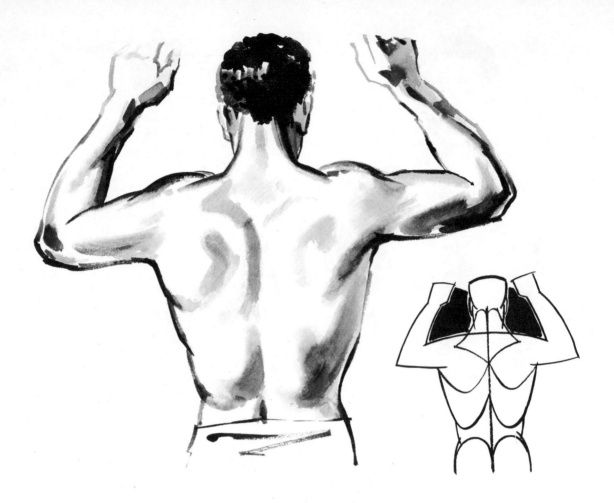

MALE TORSO (BACK VIEW)

When you start to draw your figures
remember the basic proportions on page
36 but remember also that these are
average, conventional. Visualize the three
basic mass shapes, the head, chest and
hips, and that these are all three-dimensional and hinge together. When drawing
a particular pose be clear as to what it is
you wish to portray. A relaxed pose?
Tensed? Action?

Establish the direction of the imaginary hip line and the shoulder line. Make
use of the plumb line. The figure must
be drawn from all angles and in all
positions. Sketch from life whenever
opportunity offers.

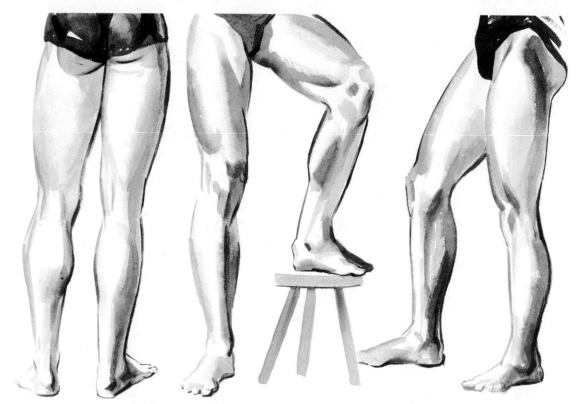

SAME POSE CLOTHED AND NUDE

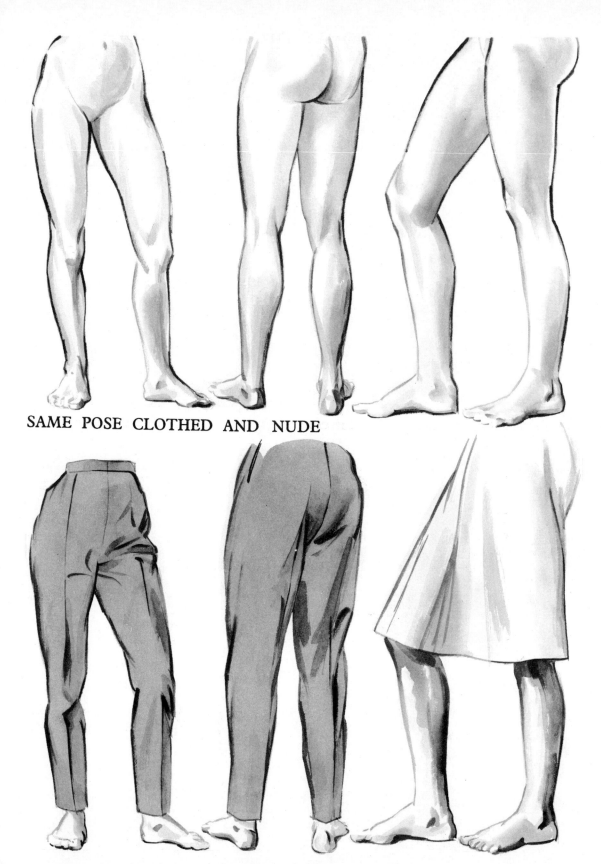

SAME POSE CLOTHED AND NUDE

FEMALE TORSO

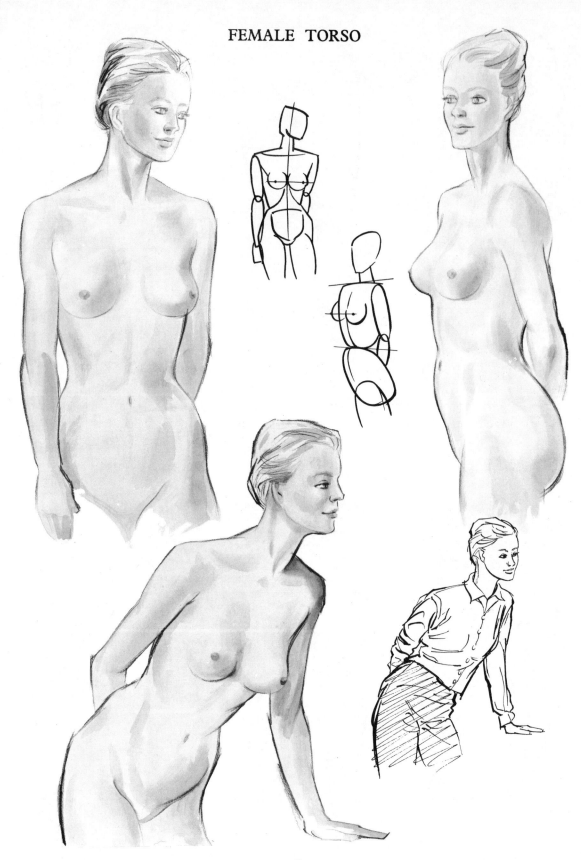

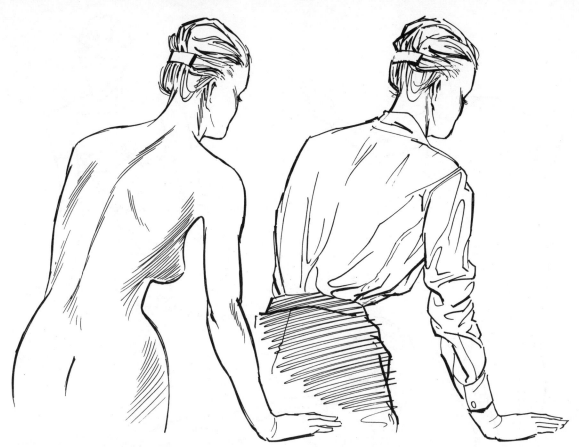

FEMALE TORSO (BACK VIEW)

Here we have built up a female back view from frame shapes (bottom right) to the nude and clothed figure. Establish the shoulder line, hip line, then the three basic shapes. Finally, we can see how the drapery is affected by the pose, moulding to the figure at some points and hanging more loosely elsewhere. Make a tracing of the clothed figure, place this on the nude form and you will see how the body affects the hang of the clothes.

The way in which the clothes hang, their creases and folds, help to express the pose and rhythm of the figure and should always be studied carefully. Note here the folds in the sleeve caused by the slightly bent arm and the almost complete absence of creases where the blouse is stretched almost taut across the back by this particular pose.

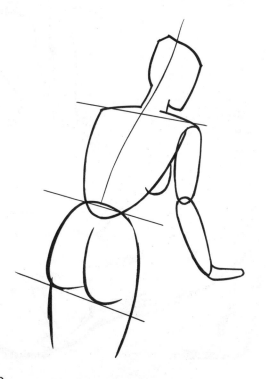

49

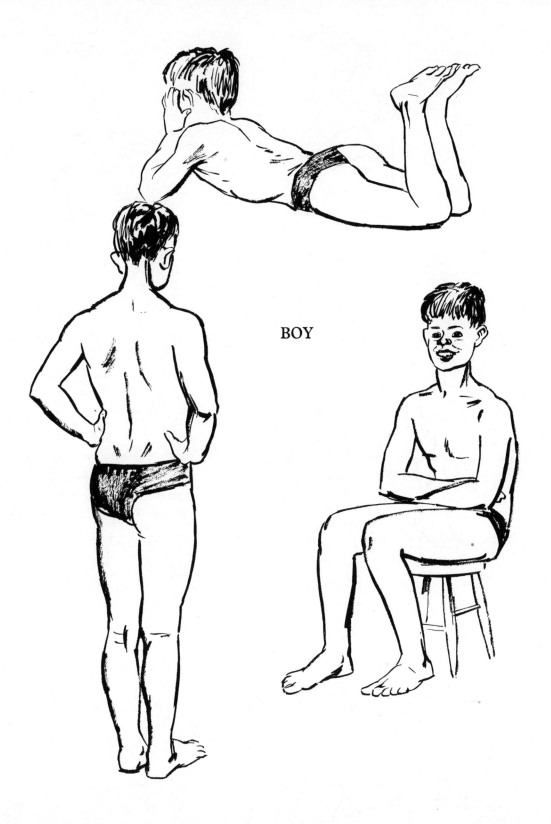

BOY

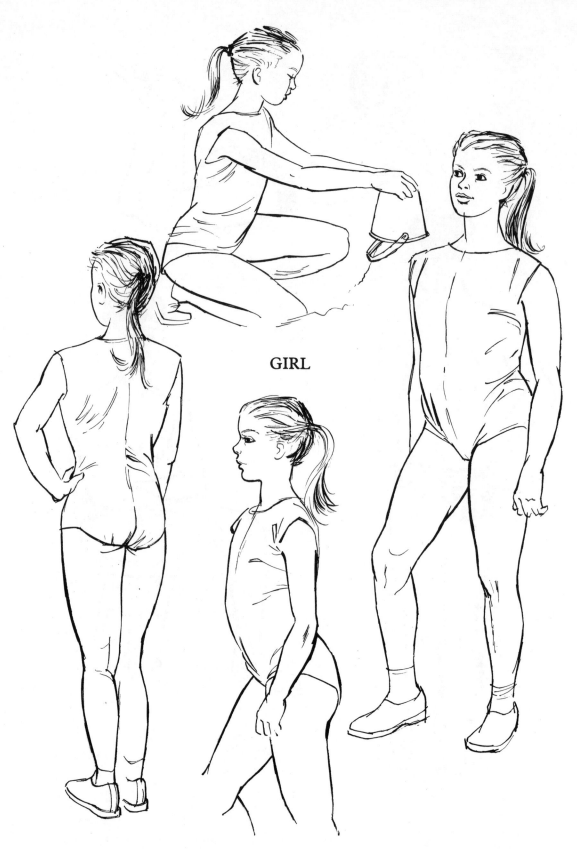

GIRL

HANDS

The palm of the hand is longer than the back, the fingers starting on the top of the hand at the knuckle bend and where the palm ends on the palm side. The first joint of the fingers is equal to the other two but on the palm side this is obscured by the palm extending half-way along the first joint.

To draw hands correctly requires much practice. Draw your own hands; use the mirror technique for drawing your left hand in different positions; draw from life as often as possible and the hands of old persons are particularly useful to study. When you first start to practise get your basic shapes and proportions, especially where fore-shortening is concerned, and remember your understanding of perspective.

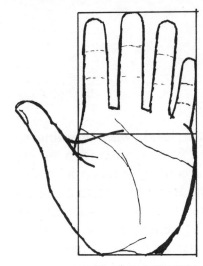

AVERAGE PROPORTION

FEET

As with the hand, when learning to draw the foot first visualize it in simple shape parts according to its position and then proceed. In profile the foot can be visualized as a triangle, and so on according to position, as the examples here. The outer base line of the foot is flat, inner side rises above ground.

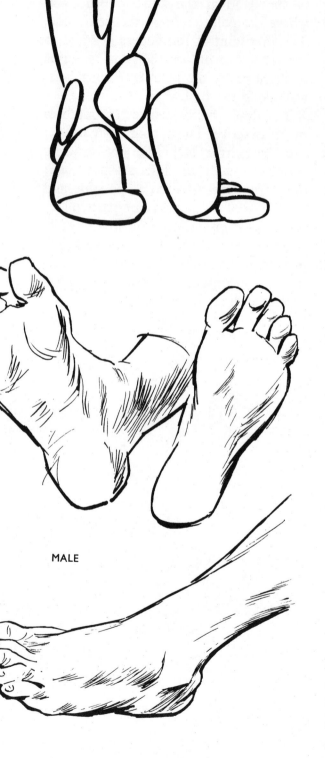

FEMALE

MALE

54

FIGURES IN RELATIVE DISTANCE AND PERSPECTIVE

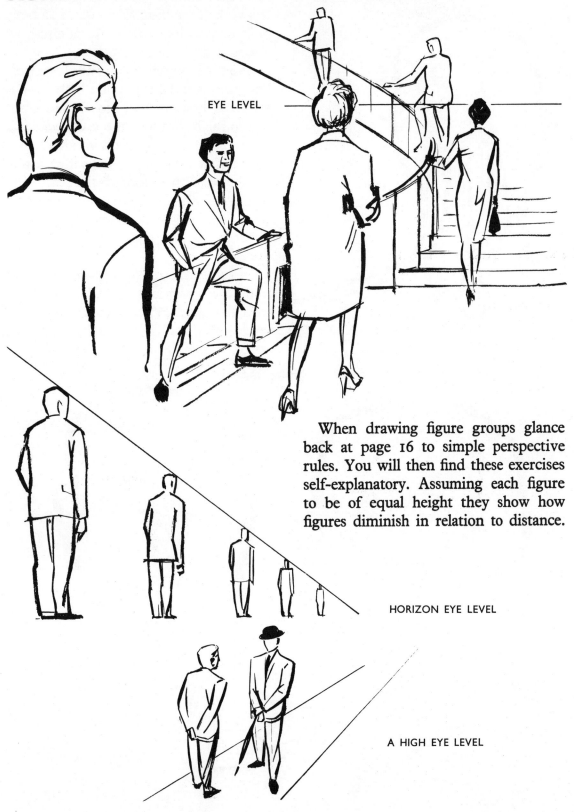

EYE LEVEL

When drawing figure groups glance back at page 16 to simple perspective rules. You will then find these exercises self-explanatory. Assuming each figure to be of equal height they show how figures diminish in relation to distance.

HORIZON EYE LEVEL

A HIGH EYE LEVEL

HEAD AND NECK

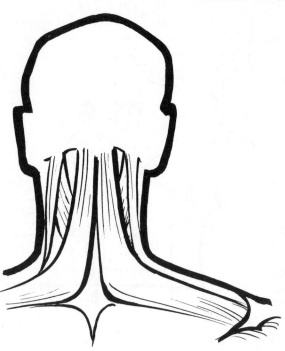

Think of the head as circular in a box; in some positions it is nearer a circle, in others oval shaped.

Basic proportion. A central vertical line gives you the mid-point between the eyes and bisects nose, mouth and chin. A central horizontal line gives you eye positions. Half-way between here and base of jaw is the base of the nose. Half-way between these levels is the centre line of the mouth. The length of the ear is from eye to base of the nose. Distance between the eyes equals the width of an eye.

In early practice of drawing the head in different positions, visualize your cube in perspective. When you draw in your circle shape and proportion lines for the

MUSCLE FORM AND BONE SHAPE

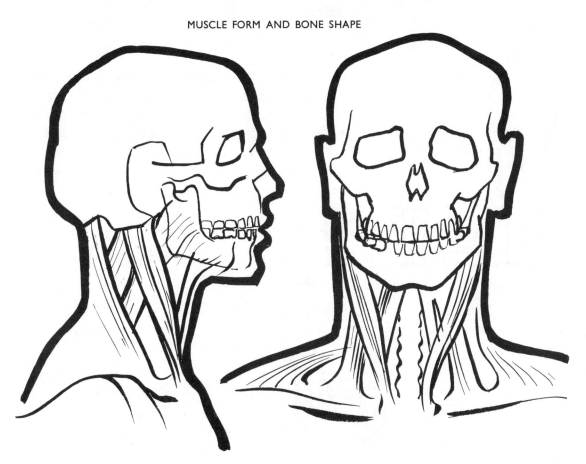

features, continue these lines around your cube or circle to complete your perspective. Observe the bone structure from the following exercises and from life studies.

Drawing the neck needs far more care than is generally given to it. The neck is cylindrical, longer in front than at the back, and its V-shaped cords turn with the action of the head. The neck inclines forward in both male and female, but is more perpendicular and thickest in the male. It is longer, more graceful and more forward-leaning in the female. In men, of course, the larynx protrudes more.

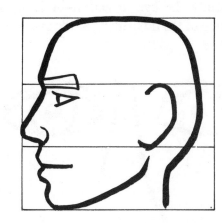

Practise sketching heads in awkward, fascinating positions. Note particularly the angle and shape of eyes and mouth; the position lines curve upward when the head looks up, downward when the head looks down.

FACE FEATURES

The features give life to your face. They also give it expression—happy, sad, stern, kindly, pensive, frightened or what you will. It is important to study their individual construction.

The eye is the most expressive. Study the shape and thickness of the eyelids and study the eye in action—raising or lowering of the lids, lifting of the eyebrow, direction of gaze.

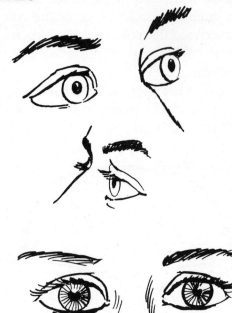

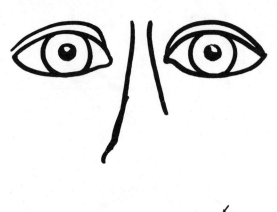

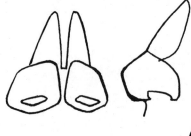

The nose is wedge shape and you should study the variety of shapes of the nostrils in different people.

The mouth is not a slit in the face but a modelled shape. Slight adjustments produce a range of expressions, notably raising or drooping the corners.

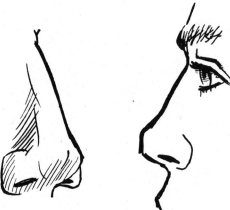

Certain shapes of mouth are associated with certain characteristics—thin straight lips for prim and proper type, thick loose lips for the greedy and sensuous, and so forth.

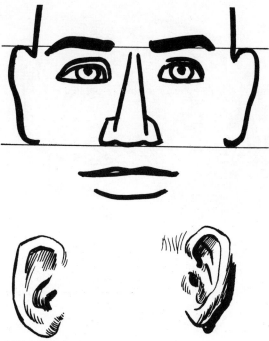

Ear shapes vary greatly. To position the ear correctly is half the battle; remember that it stretches from brow to base of the nose, and in profile it is in the centre of the head.

HEAD HINTS

Here is an idea that you may find helpful, illustrated by the two drawings below. Take two lengths of black thread each about 9 in. long and draw them over a piece of moistened gummed paper. Apply them to your face if you are drawing yourself with the aid of a mirror, or you can use a small plaster model. When turning the head into different positions you will establish proportion and position lines more easily.

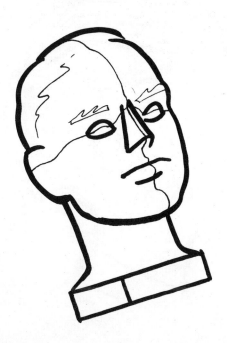

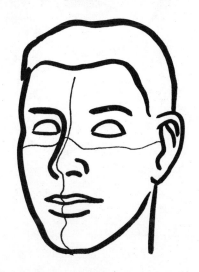

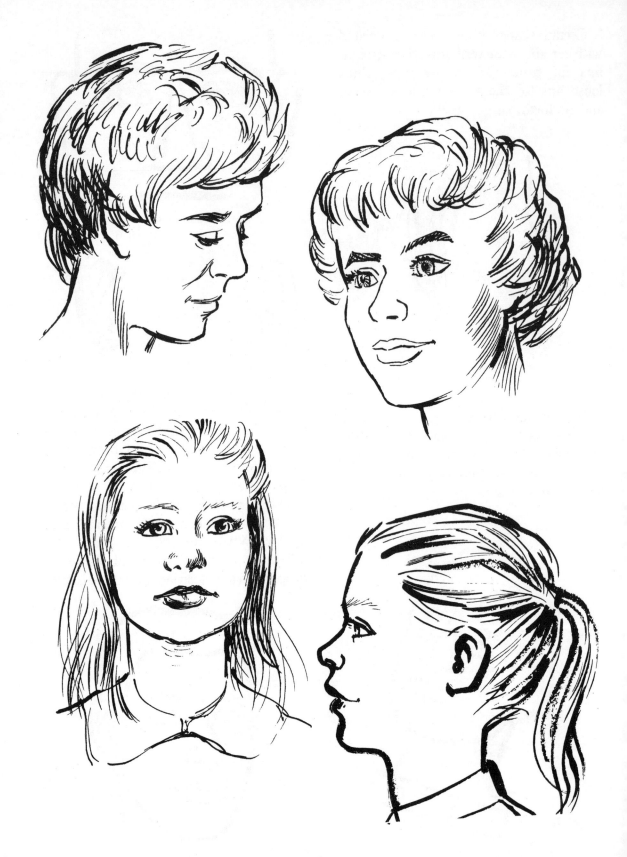

Finally, however well the head is drawn it must poise naturally on the shoulders, so make it a habit to include the neck and shoulder lines in your sketches.

After practice in accurate drawing of the head and features on Bank paper, start to use cartridge paper which has a better surface upon which to work. Use good quality pencils and have a soft india rubber and a kneeded or putty rubber handy. Keep your pencils sharp.

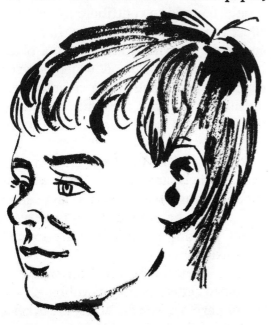

PASTEL AND
CHARCOAL DRAWING

Pastels provide an excellent way for you to experiment with colour. They are easy to use, inexpensive, and a full range of colour effects can be obtained by applying one colour on top of another. Nevertheless, practice and delicacy of touch are necessary before they can be used with skill. They are also very useful for quick sketching of fleeting colour effects such as sunsets. If you buy a box of assorted pastels you should restrict yourself to using, say, four or five colours only during early practice in order to learn the use of colour in a broad sense. Conte coloured pencils can also be used. These are called Carb-Othello pencils and they are available in a wide range of colours. In use they have a feel similar to pastel.

Charcoal is bought in sticks rather like pastel in appearance, excepting that it is black only. Charcoal drawing is for broad effects and is also useful for light sketching in outline prior to painting in water-colour a flick of the duster removes most of the charcoal and leaves only faint guiding lines. Just as Conte pencils are a pencil form of pastels or crayons, so carbon pencils can be used as well as charcoal. They produce an intensive black and are made in several grades of hardness. You will also need, of course, a good putty rubber.

Pastel or crayon, Conte pencil, charcoal and carbon pencil drawings should be fixed to avoid smudging. You should not do this, however, until you have finished your drawing, because fixative is inclined to raise the surface of the paper slightly and the application of crayon after fixing can produce a spotty effect. To fix your drawing you need a bottle of fixative and a spray diffuser. When you blow through the diffuser a fine spray results and this leaves a thin protective film over the surface of your drawing.

What sort of paper do you need? You can practise pastel drawing on almost any sort of 'not' surface paper, that is, paper which has a surface which is not smooth. This may include, especially for the beginner starting to practise, ordinary wrapping paper, the rough side of brown paper, or reverse side of M.G. paper, which can be obtained from any printer. Art shops, of course, keep a range of papers of different colours, including tinted boards, suitable for pastel work. As well as coloured papers there is a variety of grey papers, including David Cox's water-colour papers in a range of slightly varying oatmeal shades.

The grey tone of the paper, or whatever other colour the paper may be, should be used to contribute to the tone effect you are trying to achieve. In a black and white drawing you may use a black crayon, for instance, on white or grey paper; or black and white crayons on a medium-grey paper, the white crayon for highlights and both together for certain half-tone values.

As we said at the beginning of this page, pastels are an excellent way of experimenting with colours and good pictures can be produced. To preserve a pastel painting it must be glass-framed and airtight.

Extra pressure on one end will give a graded effect without rubbing, see top of page 63. For flat areas, break off a portion of the stick and hold as shown.

The middle and smaller fingers are shown below being used to smear and graduate the tone, but you must not apply too much pressure. The greater is the pressure, the more the finger is inclined to polish the surface and make further application of colour difficult as the pastel will skid over a smooth surface. Remember to finish your drawing completely, then 'fix' it as explained on page 62.

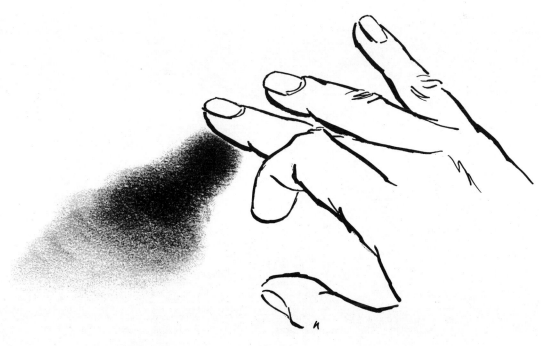

PRE-MIXING OF COLOUR

For certain effects, pastel in powder form is needed. Pare down the stick with a blade, dip the finger into the powder and mix with other colour, either on a small piece of card or on the actual sketch.

Practice and experiment will show which colours are easy to manipulate and those colours which are inclined to be coarse. Students' colours are much more gritty than artists' colours. You are advised to buy the best; choose a range of about twenty-four colours.

Paper sticks, made of soft material for fine mixing and modelling of colour on the drawing, may be purchased. Keep the same ones for particular colours as much as possible, or otherwise clean by smoothing away the tip with fine sand paper.

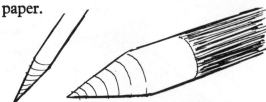

WORKING IN COLOURED PASTEL

Begin with a simple subject, say fruit or vegetables. Such a subject has plenty of colour, simple shapes, roundness and depth. Utilize the background colour of the paper as effectively as possible. Tackle your drawing boldly and try to cover a good area of your paper. Exert little pressure on your pastel, keep the tones fairly light, then lightly place your highlights. Then gradually build up deep tones, shadows and highlights to full strength.

FIRST STAGE   SECOND STAGE

Now you have decided that you will do a portrait in coloured pastel. You have selected your paper, perhaps of a buff colour. The colour of the paper will act mainly as a background, but you should avoid covering the entire head with colours and tones. The paper is itself a colour and should show in the modelling and colouring of the face and clothes. An example of such a sketch is shown below in black and white drawn on grey paper.

BLACK AND WHITE

For portrait work in black and white, again using a tinted paper, draw very faintly with an HB pencil the features and shape of the sitter. It is essential that this is done very delicately so that all traces of lead pencil are covered by the pastel. Lines made heavily with a lead pencil will cause the carbon pencil to skid. Lead pencil errors can be erased carefully with your putty rubber and the drawing commenced in carbon; should you sketch with carbon pencil only, draw your preliminary lines very lightly in white because black carbon pencil is very difficult to erase.

Use a soft black carbon pencil and a white carbon pencil, lightly indicating the highlights of the head and accentuating these to medium strength where the highlights are most pronounced. Now use your grey carbon pencil to place light modelling of shadows or dark flesh tones. Increase both whites and blacks as you proceed and to full strength where you judge that this is required.

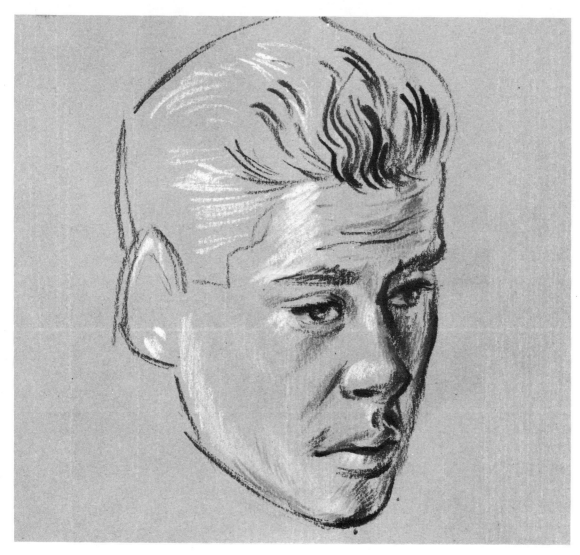

Almost any subject lends itself to the technique of pastel. If sharp edges are desired, to give a more pronounced form to certain subjects or for very clearly defined shadow effects, straight edges or cut-out shapes made from Bank paper will be of great assistance as shown in the examples here.

A black and white pastel sketch executed on a grey paper is shown overleaf, page 68.

WORKING IN INK

Drawing in ink gives opportunities for using a variety of techniques. The tones between black and white can be shown by varying the thickness of lines; by shading in parallel lines which may be horizontal, vertical or diagonal, and again these can be 'cross-matched' by lines drawn in the opposite direction; by dot stipple; by using wavy lines or other forms, sometimes the nature of the subject (i.e., texture of cloth material) helping to decide the treatment to be used; and by combining brush and pen work.

Very little practice should be necessary for you to overcome any initial tendency for your nib to scratch or dig into the paper. A range of different types of nibs—a card of Gillot nibs, for example—can be purchased for use in an ordinary penholder. Keep your nibs clean from encrusted ink. A drawing pen which works on the fountain pen principle is also available. One of these is very useful, particularly for outdoor sketching. It can be filled with Pelican black fountain pen ink, which is waterproof, and the special nibs are interchangeable and very easy to work.

When you have constructed your drawing in pencil, you should then indicate the varying tone gradations also by pencil shading, but more lightly than you would for a purely pencil drawing, so that you have on your paper or board a clear pattern of the final effect that you wish to achieve by your pen shading. When your ink work is dry, rub out the pencil foundation.

INDIAN INK (carbon black) is the ink most commonly used for black and white line drawing. It is jet black and waterproof, unaffected by rain once it is dry. Indian ink is not suitable for fountain pens as it cakes on the nib.

SEPIA INK is another waterproof ink, with excellent depth of colour, and when used in conjunction with Sepia artist's water-colour makes a very pleasing medium for sketching.

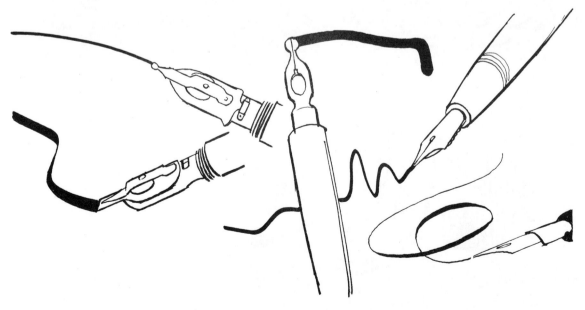

EXAMPLES OF PEN WORK

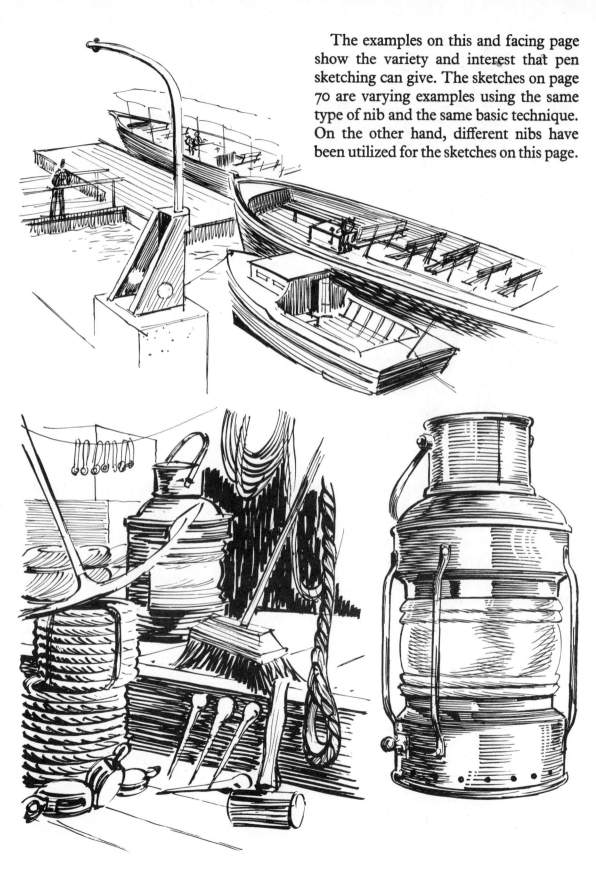

The examples on this and facing page show the variety and interest that pen sketching can give. The sketches on page 70 are varying examples using the same type of nib and the same basic technique. On the other hand, different nibs have been utilized for the sketches on this page.

We now come to ink used with brush, no pen. Though Indian ink is inclined to rot the base of a water-colour brush, a sable hair No. 2 or 3, and a 5, are needed. Whenever you are using Indian ink with your brush, immediately you stop using the brush you should wash it clean in a jar of water, particularly the base of the hairs when the ink will become encrusted if left uncleaned. This is the only way to keep your brushes in good working order, the hairs remaining flexible. Choose brushes with hairs that are fairly long, as in the Winsor & Newton Series 7. Draw freely and with vigour, at the same time lightly and sparingly, over the whole subject with your No. 2 or 3 brush. Increase your medium tones, leaving the use of your No. 5 brush until the end, when a few heavy strokes may be needed.

START   HALF-WAY   FINISH

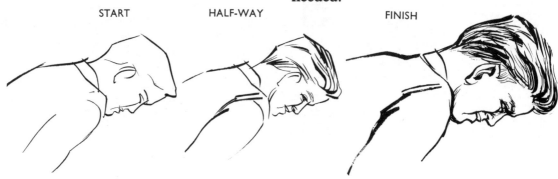

HALF-WAY   FINISH

Another way to work is by sketching certain parts, according to the nature of your drawing, with a No. 2 sable, then to work with a No. 5 or 6 sable almost dry of ink. Broad areas can thus be filled in with greyish tones. A 'not surface' paper or board is best suited to the dry brush technique, the brush sweeping over the rough surface without penetrating into the minute hollows. You can then return to your No. 2 sable for sharp detail. And remember, wash your brushes after use!

PEN AND BRUSH TOGETHER

A firm, almost continuous pen line was used to establish this scene of action. Then the brush was used to give shadow depth, to introduce half-tones, and generally to give both cohesion and movement to the whole.

INK & WATER-COLOUR

This ink sketch has the addition of Lamp Black artist's water-colour washed in varying tones to give greater depth, drama and interest to the subject. The ink, being waterproof, will not run when the water-colour is applied over it. The procedure can be reversed, but if the water-colour is applied before the ink, it must be allowed to dry before you start to use ink on the drawing.

The drawing on page 76 combines ink, using both pen and brush, with water-colour. You may wish to note here that watered-down Indian ink can be used for wash tones, but that Lamp Black artist's water-colour is more suited to this purpose. In the sketch (p.76) a heightened sense of texture has been obtained by the use of black pastel after all painting has been finished. Techniques vary from subject to subject. This sketch, and those on the preceding pages, show a few of the many ways in which you can treat a subject. Use them as a basis for the techniques they show, but use them also to stimulate your own thoughts and ideas concerning technique.

COLOURED INKS. For a small sum you can obtain a set of coloured inks from a dealer in photographic equipment. The pigment of these inks both stains and is difficult to keep under control, but to the complete extrovert to whom colour means scorching brightness at full strength, and complete freedom in its use, experimenting with coloured inks can be recommended.

PART TWO
PAINTING IN WATER-COLOURS

PAPERS AND ART BOARDS

Your chief requirement is cartridge paper; good-quality sheets are not expensive. Use thick cartridge which has a slightly rough surface and is off-white in colour. Kent 'not' paper ('not' is short for 'not pressed' surface, or rough finish) is a good paper to use. It has a crisp surface, is almost pure white, and costs a little more than cartridge paper. Another good paper is Cox's, which is oatmeal-coloured in varying shades, with a fairly rough finish which is a delightful surface on which to paint. The best quality papers, and the most used for serious work, are Whatman papers—not pressed variety, of course, for water-colours. Whatever paper you use, always buy loose sheets and cut them to the size you require.

A range of boards, paper mounted on card, is stocked by most Artists' and Architects' suppliers; their advantage being that they remain flat while you are painting and will not cockle. Surfaces vary from very smooth to fairly rough.

DRAWING BOARDS

There is a wide choice of these, from thick and heavy ones to plywood versions. Suit yourself which you buy, but it is a good idea to have an Imperial size, which measures 23 in. × 32 in., fairly substantial, and a smaller, lightweight board for outdoor sketching which could be of about half-Imperial size.

PENCIL, RUBBER, BRUSHES

An HB pencil is all that you need to sketch out the subject. A putty rubber is best used for erasing because the fine grains which rub off it when it is used do not cling to the paper, and thus the image does not become smeared by repeated brushing with the hand.

You are advised to use only pure sable brushes in water-colour painting. Purchase a range to cover your requirements. Recommended sizes of fairly long hair brushes are No. 3 (two), No. 6 (two), and one large one, say No. 9 or No. 10.

PALETTES

You can purchase palettes or dishes for mixing and using your colours, but the design of these is often far from satisfactory and they are not a necessity at this stage. You will require a palette for outdoor painting, which we will deal with later, but for the time being you will get along quite well by using saucers, enamelled plates, and similar items.

COLOURS

There are two qualities, Artists' and Students'. Artists' Colours are the best and more expensive, but Students' Colours of a reputable make are inexpensive and perfectly satisfactory with which to begin.

Water-colour paints are sold in tube

and palette form. We are not concerned with 'boxes of paints' which contain a set of colours in shallow pans in fixed positions; these have too many disadvantages for water-colour painting. Colours in palette form are like those which you get in a 'box of paints' except that you can buy a complete box, or colours individually in their palettes. However, tubes are better than palettes because they keep the paint soft and clean, ready for immediate use. In the palette form, with the paints exposed in shallow pans, the colours easily become dirty, collect grit on a windy day outdoors, and at least some of them will dry and harden.

Which colours shall you buy? The list below will cover most requirements. You may not agree with the choice; make any changes you wish but remember, when you choose your first range your first need is for strong, deep-toned colours which cannot be mixed on the palette.

MINIMUM COLOUR RANGE
- Burnt Sienna
- Burnt Umber
- Crimson Lake
- French Blue or Ultramarine
- Hookers Green Deep
- New Gamboge or Indian Yellow
- Prussian Blue
- Raw Sienna

EXTRA COLOURS TO ADD
- Brown Madder
- Cobalt Blue
- Ivory Black
- Red Ochre
- Viridian Green
- Yellow Ochre

You can add further colours to your range, as you gain experience and for obtaining special effects. From the start, cultivate the habit of always screwing the cap back on to a tube after you have squeezed the desired amount of colour from it; this is the only way to prevent your colours from getting dry and hard.

Let us now assume that you are aware of the elementary principles of colour mixing, namely that

$$Yellow + Blue = Green$$
$$Yellow + Red = Orange$$
$$Red + Blue = Violet$$

and proceed to use your colours. One final reminder; have two jars of water handy, never allow the water to get too dirty, keep your brushes clean and have a rag ready to help remove paint from a wet brush after use.

EXPERIMENTS IN COLOUR

Before starting to paint, you should experiment in mixing colours, study the effect of one colour on top of another, and note the differences between colours which appear to be alike. For example, you can see a difference between Yellow Ochre and Raw Sienna. What is the result when we mix Yellow Ochre and French Blue together in a palette, compared with laying a tint, or wash, of Yellow Ochre across a tint of French Blue? Or again, how does the result of mixing Raw Sienna and French Blue together differ from laying a tint of Raw Sienna across French Blue? This sort of experiment will help you to know your colours and to understand how to use them. Again, some colours tend to separate on the paper though they appear to mix thoroughly in the palette. Experiment with all your colours and get to know them well.

Try painting a medium-strength tint of French Blue across a tint of Yellow Ochre after the latter has dried.

Using the colours for further examples above and below, mix these together now before applying to paper in the same way and note the change in the results.

Now mix together in the palette Yellow Ochre and French Blue, apply the result to paper, and you will find that you have an effect different from the one above where the two colours have crossed in the first process. You will discover that when certain colours are mixed together they are inclined to go muddy; laid one upon another, after the first one is dry, the colour remains fresh and clean. This does not imply that colours should never be mixed together. It means simply that you must learn from experience and practice which colours to mix together, and which are best not mixed but laid one upon another separately.

We are ready with a clean sheet of paper, pinned or gum-taped to the board, a clean palette and two jars of water. The first jar is for cleaning your brush and the second is used only for mixing colours in the palette.

LAYING A WASH

When laying a wash, speed matters, so use a full brush of colour. Work freely and do not try to adhere too rigidly to boundary lines of objects; fill in the area of colour with quick strokes. This process can be repeated when your first washes are dry in order to clarify the image and record simple detail. To gradate or thin down a wash, have another palette ready with a weaker solution of the same colour; shake out a supply of water from the brush when applying a lighter tint, then let it dry. Do not go over the same place while the wash is still wet or it will dry in uneven patches.

STILL LIFE EXERCISE

For those who would prefer to know at this stage a practical method of painting, this still life study (illustrated in four stages on page 82) is explained in detail on page 83, but we suggest that you go ahead and complete the sketch in your own way, bearing in mind the principles which are given here, then compare your procedure with that described on page 83.

Make a copy of this still life group, sketching lightly with your HB pencil, to a size about 10 in. × 7½ in. Work from the top, moving across and down because you cannot lean on wet paper. Mix four palettes of pale colour for the 1ST STAGE, making sure that you mix enough to complete each wash. Work with a big brush and do not worry if one colour tends to run into another. Allow to dry. At 2ND STAGE you increase the depth of wash in the green bottle and in the foreground. Allow to dry. At 3RD STAGE, paint in the background in stronger colour with very little detail. Increase the depth of colour in the glass, in the cork in the foreground, and put light shadow on the base part of the bottle.

When dry, increase the foreground strength from the rear, gradating to lighter tone. 4TH STAGE. Increase the bottle detail to very dark as shown. Then a delicate strengthening of the glass and a broad, simple treatment for the cork. All that now remains is to strengthen slightly the shadows in the foreground, and the sketch is done. One general point to remember is to try to keep the tone values, of one object to another, light against dark.

The purpose of this exercise is to determine how well you can do at your first attempt. Of course, if you prefer to study the diagrammatic explanation on page 83 before you start, then do so. If you have been brave enough to 'go it alone'—and courage is a desirable quality in water-colour artists!—you will find it fun to retrace your steps, so to speak, and compare your procedure and colour-mixing with the one described.

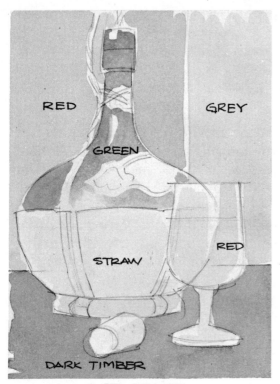

1ST STAGE
(Assume final colours to be as noted)

2ND STAGE

3RD STAGE

4TH STAGE

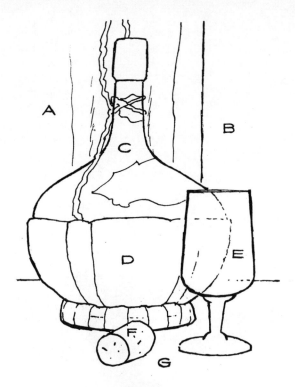

3. Show signs of Crimson Lake of background curtain. Leave highlights, increase the strength of the bottle with stronger Hookers Green Deep.

4. Paint in darker portions. Soften the edges with mix of Hookers Green Deep and Prussian Blue.

D.

1. All-over wash of Yellow Ochre.

2. Pale wash of Yellow Ochre and Ivory Black mixed, at base and right-hand side.

3. Pale wash of Light Red applied in strokes to indicate straw bands.

E.

1. Pale mix of Raw Sienna combined with a touch of Light Red.

2. Leave highlights, and increase the strength by a tint of Hookers Green Deep followed by one of Burnt Umber.

3. Pale, uneven wash of French Blue on right side of glass bowl, stem and foot.

4. Touch in fine marks on glass bowl and stem with Hookers Green Deep mixed with Crimson Lake.

F.

1. Very pale tint of Light Red.

2. Increase the depth with uneven wash of Burnt Umber.

3. Tick in cork markings.

4. Shadow and wood grain in Burnt Umber.

G.

1. Paint in the foreground with strong tone of Raw Sienna.

2. Mix Crimson Lake with Burnt Umber for stronger tone, dark in the background, lightening towards the front.

3. Finish off with a strong tone of Burnt Umber.

A.

1. Start with a pale wash of Light Red.

2. Lay a tint of Yellow Ochre.

3. Lay a stronger wash of Vermilion.

4. Lay a wash of Crimson Lake on dark folds, with touches of a mix of Crimson Lake and Prussian Blue to finish the deep shadows at base and right-hand side.

B.

1. Pale wash of French Blue.

2. Graded wash, light at the top, using Yellow Ochre.

3. Pale wash of Ivory Black.

4. Shadow of curtain, a medium-tone mix of Ivory Black and French Blue.

C.

1. Glass part of bottle, a pale wash of Raw Sienna.

2. Build up with Viridian Green on left, introducing French Blue on right to give dark side.

SIMPLE TONE PAINTING

In this exercise we are striving for complete colour control. Laying flat washes becomes more simple as you gain experience and move your brush more quickly and confidently. We now tackle a subject which is simple in shape and form but requiring split-second timing and mastery with the brush. We have three colours only, each similar in colour and tone.

RAW SIENNA
BURNT SIENNA
CRIMSON LAKE

FAWN

CRIMSON

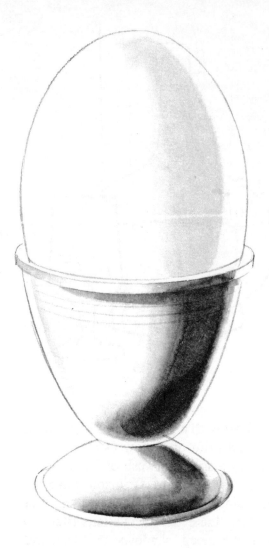

STAGE 1
Paint in shadow side first.

The purpose of the exercise is to convey as much life, solidity and colour variation as possible, making the egg realistic and third-dimensional, yet pale in tone. The egg-cup is to look shiny and translucent, and you will use only three colours. Draw and paint from life this time.

When you have completed this painting, pick any simple object in the house and try again, selecting your own colours this time but again using only three. Try your hardest to get the most out of as few colours as possible. This method will teach you two things quickly; these are colour control and the range that every colour has in itself. Repeat this procedure as often as you can, varying your subjects and choice of colours until you have utilized all the colours that you have available.

You must accustom yourself to working in darker tones with two colours at once, both wet, using two brushes for speed and control. This is essential, because your painting should not be a series of flat tones; you must get used to being able to soften and lighten the sides at the same time as you work in the deeper-toned colours.

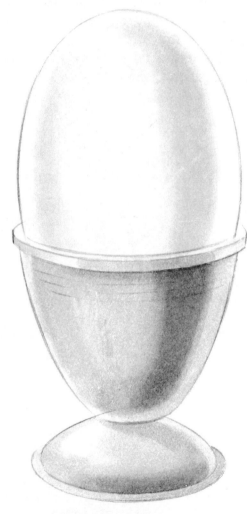

STAGE 2
Pale tint to give form.
Strong tint to give form.
Soften the edges.

STAGE 3
Pale wash all over, soften the edges.
Paint in as darkly as possible, gradate to the light on one side and the reflected light on the other

PAINTING ON WET PAPER

The purpose of painting on wet paper is to keep your colours moving together in a soft-edged woolly technique—ideal for quick sketches of furry animals.

Soak your paper thoroughly in the sink, then lay one end on your drawing board and allow the paper to roll flat. Blot off surplus water. Seal round the edges firmly to your drawing board if you intend to work 'dry' afterwards. By the way, this fastening of your paper with gummed tape instead of relying only on drawing pins is a useful device to keep in mind whenever you are painting in water-colours because it keeps your paper taut on the board when otherwise it might cockle. Continuing

with the procedure for painting on wet paper, when you have sealed the edges hold your brushes in your left hand ready for action and paint without previous drawing in pencil. You should mix separate palettes of strong colour, use one brush for each and paint swiftly. Continue to paint in swift movements with one medium-size brush until you have said all that you wish to say.

Do not touch your painting again after it has begun to dry. If you wish to add anything further, wait until the paper is absolutely dry.

This technique is tricky and needs a lot of patience and practice.

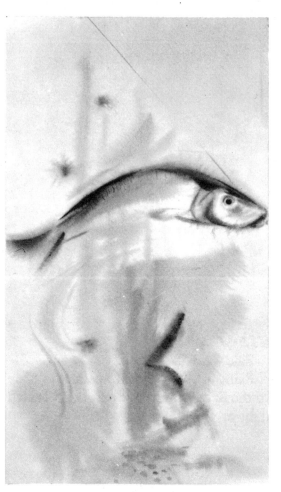

OUTDOOR PAINTING

This is the point of no return for the self-conscious artist. It is quite a bold step for the amateur to take, when he decides to stand or sit in a city main street and paint blithely away as if he has been doing it for years—when it is in fact the first time! It is sometimes said that if you are thrown into the water without first being able to swim, you will then learn—fast. In reality, you would most probably drown.

So when you first go out, find a quiet spot miles from anywhere—then paint like mad. Go out as often as you can. Do not start by trying to paint half a county. Be satisfied to start with small sketches—branches of trees, a gate, a rock sticking up out of the ground, the corner of a building, anything at all! Remember the exercises that you have done, keep the subject simple, use three or four colours only for your first attempts, and don't worry. No one will laugh at your efforts. As you gain confidence you will find that gradually all your concentrative powers are directed to your painting. You won't remember the time, nor that you are hurrying . . . you'll simply paint and keep on painting . . . that will be the great moment . . . when it arrives you will have become an artist.

EQUIPMENT

Do we walk or go by car? Keep your sketching kit light and in a convenient shape to carry because even if you go by car it will probably not take you to the actual spot where you wish to paint, and no one is happy taking awkward baggage into a public vehicle. Do not overload yourself with gear that you might need; take only what you think you will use.

SKETCH BOOK BLOCKS

These are obtainable from most art shops and a sketching block consists of a pad of sheets of good-quality water-colour paper, 'H.P.' (pressed, smooth) or 'not' (not surfaced, rough), as you prefer, sealed at the edges and bought complete with stiff backing.

Sketch blocks obviate the necessity for a drawing board and many artists prefer them for outdoor sketching. Large as well as small blocks are available so that full-sized paintings can be undertaken.

PAINTING

If you paint with a box of colours, they should be clean and ready for immediate use. If you use tubes of colour you will need a palette box such as a Winsor & Newton 'Binning Monro' box. Always return a colour to the same partition in the box so that you know exactly where to find it. Your colours should be grouped together—the yellows, browns and so forth. Two No. 3, two No. 6 and one No. 9 should comprise your sable hair brushes. A small water-bottle and a jar, an HB pencil, a knife, putty rubber and small sponge. Several sheets of paper or art board, a lightweight drawing board and a flat waterproof case in which to carry these. Two spring clips to hold your paper to the board; they are more easily used and less easily lost than drawing pins.

A final reminder concerning paper. Do not assume that a thick, heavy paper will not cockle. Outdoors a lightweight paper may be better because the wind dries the surface and a lighter paper will then flatten itself more quickly.

Assuming that several sorties into the country have been made you now feel ready to approach a more complicated subject. We will consider a general study such as a farm building together with surrounding trees and meadow land. If it is a sunny day note the position of the sun and, allowing two hours to complete your painting, estimate the final shadow position.

Sketch in lightly in pencil and determine your horizon line immediately. Do not damp your paper; your first pale wash will do this. Now to paint.

1. Lay your basic washes for the sky, say a pale mix of Yellow Ochre and Light Red. While still wet fill in the centre ground with a wash of Raw Sienna mixed with a touch of Viridian. Carry this tint to the base of the picture and add tints of very pale Vermilion for any features in the foreground area such as walls or cart tracks.

2. When the above is dry start to fill in the centre of interest section in separate stronger tones of differing shades and colours. Move forward to the foreground, using lighter washes as you do so.

3. Now back to the sky, painting in quick movements and working down to the horizon. Allow to dry. Paint in your stronger colours and shadows.

4. Complete the final details of the farm but, particularly, do not overpaint the foreground.

DRAWING WITH THE BRUSH

Your confidence is growing. So much so that this time you are going to cast away your pencil and draw as you paint with your brush. Paint in areas, each a separate pale mix of colour to establish shapes of buildings, trees, cloud form and foreground interest. Allow to dry.

Once again we emphasize the centre of interest in terms of differing colours and tones, taking each main feature separately, still working with quite a full brush and gradually building up the scene. Begin painting the sky strongly in good broad treatment. Carry on this same broad treatment in the centre parts. When quite dry paint in the main detail, including shadows. Allow to dry. Work more finely again on the centre of interest and fade to the foreground.

This method of painting without drawing the subject is a great morale builder. It helps you to paint quickly and broadly, with a nicely wet brush, and this is a good thing. No more tickling with a half-dry brush. Water-colour means WATER-colour; tickling is for scratching.

You should try to obtain a tripod easel with a board that can be fixed to the top; this will enable you to paint standing, always to be preferred, and give you greater freedom of movement. And always remember that the depth and beauty of water-colour painting lies in the earlier transparent washes that can still be seen when the painting is finished.

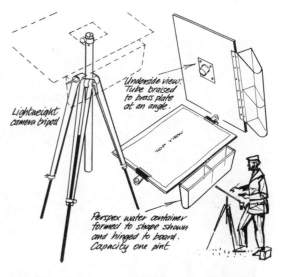

Underside view: Tube braised to brass plate at an angle.

Lightweight camera tripod

TOP VIEW

Perspex water container formed to shape shown and hinged to board. Capacity one pint

PAINTING WITH GOAUCHE COLOURS

Goauche colours are a more intense form of Poster Colour and, in a sense, they can serve as a beginner's 'Oil Colours' in that one colour has the capacity to obliterate another. When mixed to a normal creamy consistency they are quite opaque except for such colours as Primrose and Viridian Green. They are extremely finely ground and of very high quality.

The essence of water-colours is their transparency; oils, of course, are completely opaque; Goauche colours, normally opaque. Goauche colour when watered down becomes transparent and is admirable for the usual techniques employed in water-colour painting. Advantages of Goauche colours used in this way are that they dry very quickly when this is desired, and you can achieve stronger, sunnier effects with them.

PART THREE
PAINTING IN OILS

Today more people than ever before are turning to painting as a hobby, both in water-colours and in oils. Many famous people paint, and very competently, too, as a form of mental relaxation, finding oil painting particularly satisfying and, perhaps, good fun. Such hobbyists have no grand ideas concerning their ability, nor do they seek to prove anything to anyone; to paint is enough.

Painting in oils has a particular fascination. And an impressive-looking picture can be produced in oils with less skill probably than would be required for working in water-colours. With oils, you can remove paint and brush strokes if you make a mistake or change your mind and alter that part of your picture without impairing the result. When using water-colours, as you should now know, the luxury of making mistakes or changing your mind is hardly permitted. Again, water-colours are light and fresh, transparent in tone with the different colours less intense than in real life. Oils, on the other hand, are full-bodied, richer colours and with them you can render a fuller range of life-like tone values. Painting in oils means freedom of expression to many whose daily work is humdrum routine, lacking real interest or excitement. Through this medium of painting, the bus driver and the politician find a common outlet for expression.

The handyman can build his own easel, make his own paint box and palette, prepare his own art boards, so that painting in oils is not necessarily an expensive hobby. This short section of this book is written primarily for those who wish to develop a little talent in this medium and who have the time in which to do it. So with this thought in mind let us see what materials are needed and roughly how much they will cost, bearing in mind that only the best colours and brushes are good enough.

You will need paint, brushes, a palette, palette knife, charcoal, containers for turpentine and linseed oil, a box in which to keep all these things, and an easel. If you wish to be really tidy and compact, your box can be made so that it will include a couple of art boards. You can, of course, purchase oil-colour boxes fitted complete with these items. These range from the small tin-box type containing all the items mentioned, including turpentine and linseed oil but not canvas or art boards, and costing less than three pounds, to a well-fitted oil-colour box in the form of a combined box and portable painting table and easel, easily carried for outdoor work, and costing about sixteen pounds.

When working at home you will require space where the natural light is good and where you can safely leave your equipment. And it is a good idea to keep the door of the room closed or the whole house may seem to smell of linseed oil! Working with oils can also be a messy business, so wear old clothes or a smock of some kind.

We will assume that you propose to confine yourself at the beginning to purchasing only these colours and items of equipment needed to get you started in a modest way, so let us now consider these separately.

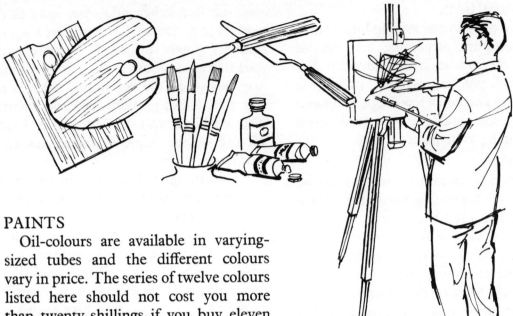

PAINTS

Oil-colours are available in varying-sized tubes and the different colours vary in price. The series of twelve colours listed here should not cost you more than twenty shillings if you buy eleven small tubes plus a larger 4-inch tube of white. A larger tube of white is necessary because it is used to dilute other colours. Purchase the following colours and use only these to start.

YELLOW OCHRE	BURNT SIENNA
CADMIUM YELLOW	FLAKE WHITE
LEMON YELLOW	FRENCH ULTRAMARINE
IVORY BLACK	COBALT BLUE
CADMIUM RED	VIRIDIAN GREEN
ALIZARIN CRIMSON	OLIVE GREEN

BRUSHES

To begin, buy one type and shape of brush. The hog-hair oval-tipped Filbert bristle type will suit your purpose. You will need eight or twelve to start painting so purchase two each of Nos. 2, 3, 6, 7, 8 and 12, which should cost about fifty shillings. You will also need a No. 3 or 4 long-haired sable for detail work and an ordinary 1-inch decorator's brush for painting in backgrounds or tinting your canvas before commencing to paint.

As you gain experience you can buy other types of brushes to suit your own needs.

PALETTES

Your palette should be not less than about 14 in. × 10 in. and a rectangular palette of this size will cost about ten shillings. Oval-shaped palettes of this size cost around fifteen shillings and are more popular, being comfortable to work with and better balanced. You can easily make your own palette from a piece of plywood or hardboard primed and surfaced with a neutral tint. Whether you buy or make your palette it should be of a size to fit your paint box.

EASEL

A wood tripod easel, with a sliding piece to grip the top of the canvas or board and hold it firmly in position, is a robust type and convenient for carrying about with you. A good sketching easel is usable both at home and outdoors. Remember to clean off paint and dirt after use or you may find the sliding parts immovable the next time you go out to paint.

OIL MEDIUMS

To simplify colour mixing buy a small bottle of pure turpentine and one of linseed oil from an artists' supplier. Fill the small palette reservoir two-thirds with turps and add a few drops of linseed oil. This mix is all that you really need for thinning your paint.

VARNISH

Retouching varnish is used to increase the tones of a painting where these have gone dull and lost their depth; it should be applied very lightly only when the paint has dried, which may be a week later. The varnishing proper of the whole picture must not be done until the paint has fully dried and hardened and this may take six months. Avoid using too much linseed oil in painting; it is slow drying and slippery.

CHARCOAL

This is for sketching in the subject. If desired, your charcoal outlines can be fixed by spraying lightly with charcoal fixative solution as described earlier in the pastel drawing section. Buy a fairly hard charcoal.

PALETTE KNIFE

This is for mixing and scraping off and a flat shape is more useful than the trommel type. You can also paint with your palette knife just as you do with a brush; painting with a knife is for broad effects—for example, a still evening sky, or for special techniques where paint thickness is required.

CANVASES AND BOARDS

For your first efforts a few off-cuts of hardboard are adequate, but the board should first be treated to prevent the colours from drying too quickly and thus making brushwork difficult. Two coats of white emulsion paint will suffice and you can use either side—you may find the reverse side of the hardboard ideal with its rough surface. It is not a bad idea to confine yourself to 14 in. × 10 in. size boards in the beginning. This is a fair size, allowing room for experiment, also enabling you to see round your picture at the subject which you are painting.

Oil painting surfaces can be obtained ranging from prepared canvas and canvas boards to hardboard panels, oil boards and oil sketching paper. Hardboard panels, rough or smooth surfaces and primed with Titanium White ready for use, cost about three and sixpence each in the 14 in. × 10 in. size. Flax canvas is made in several grain finishes and practice and experience must be your guide. At this stage confine yourself to one size and type of painting surface and leave further experiment until a later date. Always keep several boards or canvases ready primed for use.

CANVAS PINS

These are double-pointed wood pins and they are most useful for carrying wet canvases. If you always carry at least two canvases of one size, you can stack one against the other and separate them by a canvas pin in each corner, in this way carrying the wet canvas safely.

CARE OF EQUIPMENT

Keep your paint box clean and the correct caps screwed on your paint tubes. Always scrape your palette free of all paint and wipe clean with turps. Brushes should be cleansed in clean turps, then wash thoroughly with soft soap; rub the bristles firmly in the palm of the hand until all traces of colour are gone. And don't forget your soft rags; always have one with you.

EXERCISES IN PAINT

Now the fun begins. Squeeze a little colour from each tube and group together the yellows, blues, reds and so forth. With a medium size brush mix a yellow with French Ultramarine and with another brush mix the same yellow with Cobalt Blue. Pair up other colours in this way and you will quickly learn the properties of one colour relative to another.

Accustom yourself at the same time to holding the brush well away from the ferrule end, almost at right angles to your canvas. Don't be niggardly with the paint, vary your brush strokes and remember that you have six to eight brushes in your left hand—it is easy to forget that these are about 12 inches long and covered in paint! Keep each brush for a particular colour mix to avoid having to clean your brushes while you are working.

Next, introduce white with your colours. Place strokes or patches of colour together and notice how colours of a similar tone tend to dazzle while light and dark tones give contrast. Then work one colour mix with another, grading these together to give graduated tones. When the paint is dry make notations in pencil to remind you which colours were used to produce the various greens, oranges and browns; keep these first sketches by you as you will find them helpful for some time to come.

Yellows, blues and reds have their associated 'grey' shadow tones and grey is very important. Grey is in effect a mixture of yellow, blue and red. Use of Viridian Green supplies the blue and yellow, and mixed with a red will give you grey. The particular red used will determine the shade of grey, just as a touch of yellow will give you a brownish grey, or a little Cobalt will produce a cool grey. As with all colour mixing, experiment and experience will increase your knowledge.

Now enough of this! We will tackle our first subject, a Still Life, something simple and colourful such as fruit or vegetables.

STILL LIFE

First take the whiteness from the canvas or from whatever painting surface you are using, with a light colouring of Yellow Ochre or Burnt Sienna well diluted with turps and rubbed on with a rag or a 1-in. brush. This tint will suit our particular study and it should be done the day before you start your painting. Then sketch in your subject in charcoal.

Another method of working is to indicate in flat shapes all the objects included in the subject, in light complementary colours thinned with turps and using no outline at all.

You have squeezed an amount of each colour on to your palette, more of white than the other colours, grouped in a logical order and leaving you enough space for colour mixing, your thinning medium of turps plus a little linseed oil is ready and you have a selection of brushes in your left hand—so now go to work. Do not be afraid of using plenty of colour, checking shape and contour of each object to get accurate drawing and depth, remembering that you do not build up from light to dark tones in stages as in water-colour but apply your full range of tones as you proceed, finally adding the highlights.

Having done your best at a complete subject confine yourself next time to one vegetable or fruit, say an apple. Try painting the apple using as much variety of yellows and greens as possible to give a luminous effect. This means getting as much change and depth of colour as you can, keeping the tone value natural and retaining the full roundness and fruitiness of the subject. Be deliberate with your brush strokes and try to follow the contour and shape of your subject as you paint. Try to get almost pure dark blues in the shadow parts, using both Cobalt and Ultramarine.

Now compare this little study with your first group. There should be quite a difference; the first study may look flat and lifeless in comparison. You will realize that a simple subject such as a tomato is not just one flat colour graded from light to dark; it is many reds, blues and yellows painted one within another. Painting studies like these will open a new world of colour for you; experiment as much as possible and you will learn much from your experience.

After these experiments, next try a more tricky subject such as flowers in a bowl. Again try to avoid using one green for all the leaves; remember the apple. Work fairly broadly, avoid the danger of becoming finicky at this stage and remember that highlights and detail should be worked up to gradually cover the whole painting. Never finish one part completely. Leave the highlights until the end.

LET'S GO OUT

Some time will elapse before you venture out into the open to paint. But sooner or later you must take the plunge, so start to observe as much and as often as you can, everything you see around you. The shapes of buildings, the fascinating natural compositions of objects and buildings. You will notice details that you have previously passed several times without realizing that they were there. Note the texture of things, too, because colour and correct tone are not always sufficient in themselves in the portrayal of buildings.

With so many aspects to bear in mind a good deal of observation is necessary apart from actual painting; therefore you should consider your subject at some length before you start to paint.

The tackling of an architectural subject requires careful planning. You are advised to indicate in thin paint, using a small brush, the horizon line and all the essential lines of direction. Paint in block form large areas in a thin mixture of Burnt Sienna and Cobalt Blue to indicate the shadow side, so that the whole picture is clearly indicated in general shape and light direction. At this stage your picture will look almost like a setting of toy bricks. With this as your basis you can fill in your medium tones in the correct colours, paint in your lighter parts, then the shadow side. Afterwards more detail can be added.

Work vigorously, allowing your brush strokes to follow perspective angles and uprights. Background parts should be treated very simply and in a lighter tone to convey distance. Try to complete your sketch within two hours because the light direction will be changing and you should endeavour to estimate its final position within that time. Architecture will always remain a wonderful subject for colour.

PAINTING LANDSCAPES

Landscapes set a special problem because of the preponderance of greens. All sorts of greens – yellow ones, blue and brown ones, and some that are hardly green at all. The problem is further aggravated by the hazard of light, which is constantly changing.

A panoramic view presents the worst

kind of 'greens' problem—a never-ending patchwork. Leave this type of painting until you have had plenty of practice. Simplify your early subjects by attempting more condensed arrangements such as the two shown on these facing pages, or you can try a scene which is even more of a close-up and consisting almost entirely perhaps of a single dominating tree, with someone sitting in the shadows. How do we start?

First, we fix the horizon line whether or not we can see it. We then mark out the subject with a brush to get correct proportion in all the elements of the painting. Look at the sky and back-ground as one; the sky can help to show up interesting background features. If the sky is moving rather quickly have several small quantities of colour ready, using different brushes. Now paint in the whole sky as quickly as you are able to do so, capturing the movement completely.

If you wish you can now clean your palette and mix several tones of green, then quickly establish the shape and colour of the trees. Paint in your bridge or other main feature, then move on to the foreground. Here, your greens can afford to lose themselves a little, by this we mean that they can be quite pale and

soft in colour, or strong but very simple, using a broad open treatment. Never labour the foreground or overdo the colour.

If a tree or some other object not seen in your painting throws a shadow on the foreground, paint in the shadow; it will help to convey a feeling of greater space. Do not overdo the tone but allow it to sink into and become a part of the foreground.

Lastly, it is not necessary to follow rigidly the colours that you see before you. Your own interpretation of what you see can be expressed in any way you choose. Visit art galleries as often as possible and study the works of others; in doing so you will learn much that is not described here. Many great painters of the past, and others almost unknown, have portrayed the landscape scene so well and in such interesting ways that you cannot afford to miss a single opportunity to see and study their work.

PORTRAIT PAINTING

If portrait painting is of special interest to you these notes may help you to avoid the more common errors. You should be a good painter of still life subjects before you can expect to achieve worthwhile results in portrait painting.

PLACING
Place the head and shoulders nicely within the area of the canvas. You may prefer a side view as being easier to start with; later you will try a three-quarter front view and then your problems will really begin.

PROPORTION
To achieve accurate proportion, paint in quickly the whole outline of the figure to be painted, then check your measurements with the model to see that the head is drawn to the correct size. Establish the position of the eyes in relation to the base of the nose as though seen through a triangle. Carefully indicate the position and depth of the ears and eyebrows.

PERSPECTIVE
Although the head is small, perspective must be taken into account, especially the 'lie' of the eyes and the angle of the mouth. Seen in perspective, one eye is a little larger than the other, one side of the mouth shows more than the other. The angle and depth of the nose must look right.

LIKENESS AND COLOUR
Do not be disappointed if you fail to produce a good likeness at your first attempt; indeed, try more to get the feeling of the subject, the person, into your painting. Flesh tones vary but, generally speaking, try to avoid pink as such—that is to say, red and white alone.

DETAIL AND BACKGROUND
Work up the painting as a whole. Leave details, such as those of nostrils, eyes and final lip shape, until towards the end. Try to concentrate the interest mainly in the head; clothes should be added only to give a realistic look to the figure but, normally, you should not embroider with too much detail. Keep the background simple but nicely textured.

PART FOUR
COMMERCIAL ART

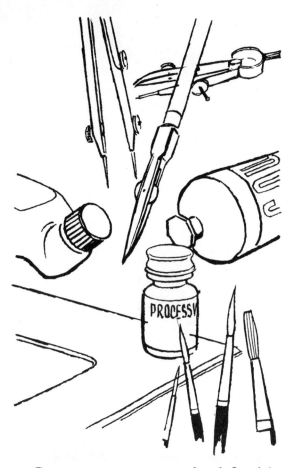

COMMERCIAL ART may be defined in practical terms as drawing and designing for commercial purposes in the form of newspaper and magazine advertisements and editorial illustrations, book jackets, posters, showcards, letterheads, folders, brochures, and in a broader sense it includes work such as designs for wallpapers and textiles. The commercial artist should be aware of two general principles which govern his work.

The first is that he is not selling art but using it to sell something else—a product or service, or even an idea. It is this product, service or idea that matters most. If this principle seems that it must deflate the artist's ego and act contrary to natural artistic expression, such an assumption would be a mistaken one. There is opportunity to develop individualistic skills, scope for originality, and a wide field of work in which the competent artist can enjoy an honest pride in his craftsmanship.

The second principle is that the commercial artist's work is only as good as its reproduction. This means that the artist should have a knowledge of the technical processes by which his work is reproduced in printed form, so that his drawing technique and the materials that he uses are suited to the kind of printed reproduction for which his work is intended.

This section of the book introduces the student to commercial art on the basis of these two principles. It cannot be more than an introduction, in the same way that the first 100 pages explain the basic principles of drawing and painting in a general way. It is hoped that this section can provide a groundwork upon which the commercial artist can build a career for himself by further study and, above all, by continual practice.

The basis of all art is the same; an understanding of perspective, light and shade, composition, the use of colour and so forth. But commercial art in its basic form demands exactness, careful finish whether it is in ink, wash or colour. If you are doing a line drawing of an egg-beater which is to appear as part of an advertisement, it must be exactly as the manufacturer makes it and not just any old egg-beater. It must be as exact as a photograph but clearer in detail. The lines and shading technique must be precisely drawn, definite in application and carefully finished. A modest subject well drawn, and executed with a knowledge of commercial art techniques, is marketable; a gallant attempt at a difficult subject which is not drawn sufficiently well, and using amateurish techniques, is not so likely to recommend you to a Commercial Art Studio. Do not be afraid of being modest in your aspirations; be proud of being competent in whatever it is that you attempt to do.

Your initial training and your own inclinations will gradually determine the way in which you will develop as a commercial artist—as a figure artist, lettering specialist, skilled in scraperboard work, all-rounder, poster-artist, still life or fashion artist—so let us have a look at the opportunities open to you and ways of entering the wide field of commercial art.

A COMMERCIAL ART CAREER offers many opportunities of employment by advertising agencies, art studios, manufacturing firms, department stores, printers, blockmakers, exhibition stand designers and television studios, or you may be a free-lance. The beginner who leaves school without any special art training, or the student who has spent three or four years at an art school or technical college but who has had no practical experience, often finds it more difficult to get themselves started in a commercial art career than they had supposed. Why is this?

Your first realization must be that, with or without initial art training, you must start as a beginner. An advertising agency's studio, or a department store's advertising department, though sometimes quite large, is generally a relatively small and skilled unit and its intake of artists who are absolute beginners in the commercial field must be limited. The other main reason is that students who

have had training at an art school often present themselves at commercial studios, seeking a post, with samples of work which are far removed from commercial reality. All forms of art may have the same foundation but, as suggested here already and explained in the pages that follow, *commercial* art requires a working knowledge of various commercial media, or materials, ability in specific commercial art techniques, and an understanding of reproduction methods. If as an art student you intend eventually to enter the commercial field, be very sure that your studies include, as well as basic drawing training, instruction in current commercial techniques. A career in commercial art can be interesting, satisfying and financially rewarding.

A REFERENCE FILE is required by every commercial artist; once you have started to compile one you should add to it continually. There are several classification methods and one simple way is to keep the cuttings and photographs in a series of large labelled envelopes, filed in alphabetical order. These may be labelled 'Animals', 'Hands', 'Buildings', 'Ships', 'Scraperboard styles', 'Layout', 'Lettering', 'Farming', and so on. If you are suddenly required to draw an old windjammer you would be glad of a comprehensive 'Ships' file; and a good way of improving your own scraperboard technique is to study as many different styles as possible in a collection of such reproductions. A reference file is both a source of factual pictorial information, which a commercial artist needs for his drawings to be accurate, and a springboard for creative ideas.

BEGINNER'S MATERIALS

Smooth cartridge paper.

Bottle of Indian Ink.

Pot of Process White.

12-in. rule.

Ruling Pen, and ordinary pen holder and nib.

8-in., 45° Set Square.

Pair of Dividers.

Pair of Compasses, with ruling pen attachment.

Nos. 2 and 3 Sable Hair Brushes (long hair).

So far as line drawings are concerned, the nature of the drawing mostly determines the result which a reduction in size will produce. Some line drawings reduce to a fraction of their original size without any loss of detail. But line drawings which contain tints laid on the artwork (see page 107), or other fine shading lines, cannot be greatly reduced unless one can visualize and is prepared for the probable result—that the tints and shading lines may come too close together as to almost disappear and merge into an overall darker effect.

A line drawing that requires two or more colours for its printing is prepared in a special way and this is described in the printing and blockmaking sections at the end of the book. This is multi-colour line work. Artwork which is reproduced by line methods, as opposed to drawings which are reproduced by half-tone, include all drawings in clear black and white (usually in black ink) and all colour drawings where only flat colours are used without any tone gradations.

When drawing in ink for line reproduction you should ensure that all your pen or brush masses, lines and dots that compose your drawing are really black—and not grey. This helps the blockmaker and guarantees a good reproduction.

ADVANCED MATERIALS

Kent paper; smooth and not surface.

Bristol Board for fine line work.

Scraperboard for extra fine work and special effects.

Fashion Boards; smooth, not, and rough.

Kodatrace for multi-colour line work.

Self-adhesive tints (there is a wide range of these).

Tin of rubber-solution.

Pen and pencil spring-bow compasses.

Gillot's No. 290 pen nibs for fine line work.

Gunther Wagner pen with choice of interchangeable nibs for most types of line work

Pelican fountain pen ink.

Drawing board and T square.

Tracing paper.

4H pencil for tracing down.

There are many techniques used in commercial art, especially in line work, and these techniques are constantly changing and improving. You should study the illustrations in advertisements and, using the knowledge gained from this book, try to understand how the various effects are achieved.

Artwork which is intended for reproduction is usually drawn larger than its published size. This makes drawing easier for the artist and a sharper image is produced when the drawing is photographed to a size which is smaller than the original. It is customary to execute the artwork 'half-up' on its intended printed size, that is half as large again. But all general rules may sometimes be broken and occasionally for special reasons it is necessary to prepare a drawing several times larger than what is to be its printed size.

LINE DRAWING TECHNIQUES

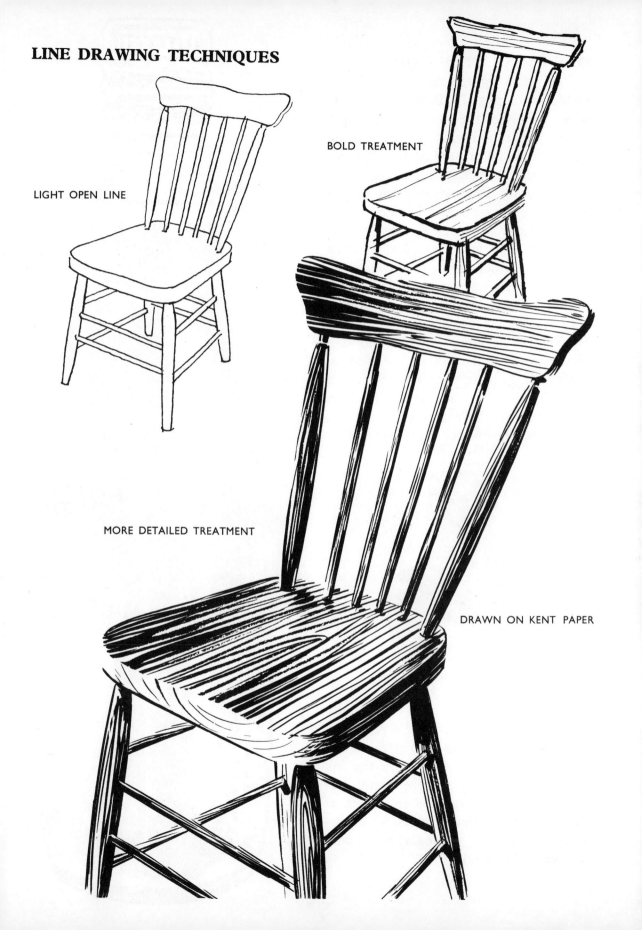

LIGHT OPEN LINE

BOLD TREATMENT

MORE DETAILED TREATMENT

DRAWN ON KENT PAPER

DRY BRUSH TECHNIQUE

You were introduced to dry brush technique on page 73. In commercial art it is a very effective way of producing a strong illustration which is meant to be reproduced and printed on poor quality paper, such as newsprint, though it is also used for illustration work in the glossy paper magazines. Fashion pages of the Sunday newspapers generally contain one or two examples of this technique, either used alone or in combination with other techniques to increase the dramatic effect of the whole. Dry brush work is generally reproduced from a line negative. Practice and skill are necessary so that you do not produce too much 'grey' in your work which, if your drawing is to be reproduced from a line and not from a screen negative, will either reproduce black or not at all.

DRAWN ON ROUGH SURFACED BOARD

For this work the use of partially worn brushes Nos. 2, 5 and 6 is recommended. Ink is inclined to streak when used in this way, as shown in the ink bottle drawing. The sauce bottle was drawn in red poster colour, which is easier to work with and which for reproduction purposes photographs equally as well as black ink.

FINE LINE WORK AND USING MECHANICAL TINTS

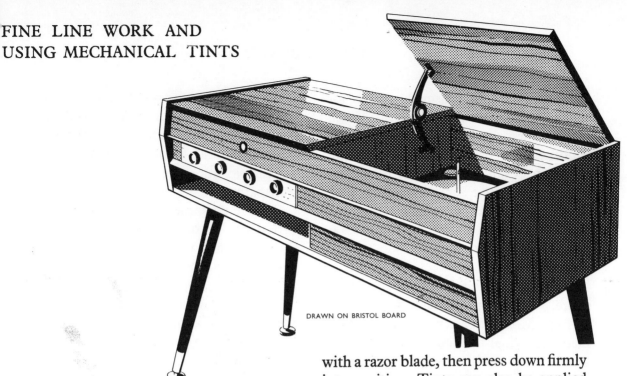

DRAWN ON BRISTOL BOARD

All the line work is drawn with a ruling pen and the broken lines are touched out by using a brush and process white paint. Curved lines are drawn with a No. 1 brush. A self-adhesive mechanical tint is used for the shaded parts.

Self-adhesive tints of various kinds are obtainable from Artists' Suppliers. These are used in drawings for line reproduction to give tone and shadow effects; the backing is removed from the thin transparent sheet on which the tint is printed, then the tint is simply pressed down on to the drawing. If the tint is to cover an awkward shape, press down lightly on to the drawing a slightly larger piece than required, cut to shape with a razor blade, then press down firmly into position. Tints can also be applied during blockmaking when the drawing is being photographed for reproduction, and this is explained in the printing and blockmaking section.

On this page are a few examples of self-adhesive tints. They must be used with care, especially if the drawing is to be reduced in size when being photographed for reproduction. When selecting the tint an allowance must be made for the effect of such reduction.

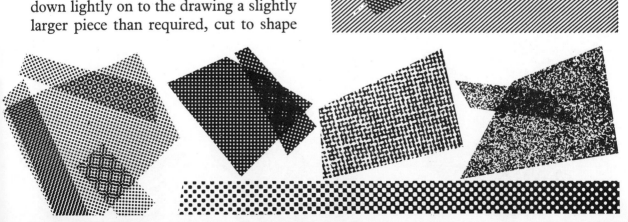

SCRAPERBOARD

Scraperboard is normally used for very fine line work of great detail. When it is for newsprint reproduction a broader treatment is generally used but no rigid rules can be given. No other technique reproduces better on newsprint than scraperboard and you should collect and study scraperboard work cut from newspapers and magazines.

EQUIPMENT

Scraperboard is sold in sheets—plain white, black, or grained for special effects. Most experienced users have their individual methods and tools. You should start with a lightweight knife,

sharp-angled to a point, one or two scraperboard nibs (these fit on ordinary pen holder), long-haired sable brushes Nos. 1, 2, and 3, black Indian Ink, a 45° plastic transparent set square and a transparent rule.

Start in a simple way by drawing lines with a pen or brush, then scrape across them to obtain various effects. Use your pen or brush smoothly and with an even flow of ink; you are working on a polished surface which scratches easily, and you must allow the ink to dry completely before you start to use your scraper tool.

VARIOUS SCRAPER EFFECTS

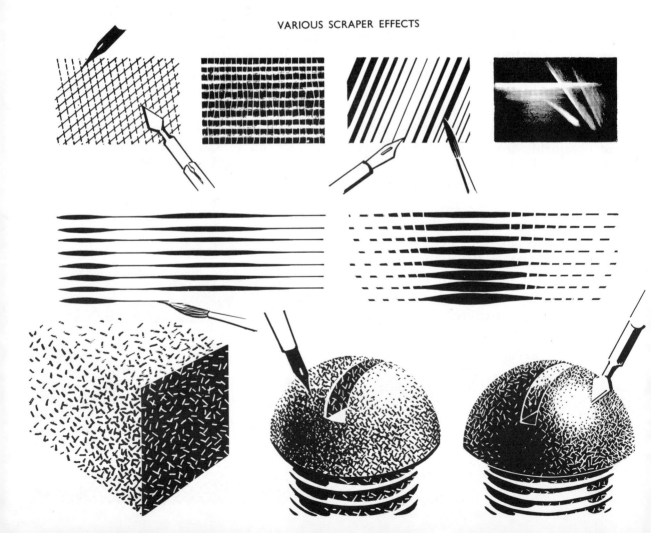

For long, slow-curved lines that vary in thickness, use a brush against the upturned edge of your ruler.

Slope your brush forward, then move it through an upright position to a backward sloping angle as you proceed with the stroke. Uneven pressure will increase or decrease the line thickness.

In scraperboard drawing, any one of a wide range of treatments may be used, from a free style method to precision techniques which are almost mechanical in their appearance, so that widely different results are achieved by means of this one medium. Many scraperboard drawings where a careful technique is used are based on photographs—heads, figures, intricate engineering subjects—to give a clearer, more dramatic presentation than would a reproduction from the actual photograph itself. Again, textures as different as wool, wood or glistening glass can be realistically presented by a scraperboard technique, so that in advertising art a scraperboard drawing may be used to illustrate anything from a tweed jacket to a suite of furniture, a metal container, or a pair of socks.

THREE SCARPERBOARD STYLES:
SIMPLE, CAREFUL TECHNIQUE
PRECISION TREATMENT
FREE STYLE TREATMENT

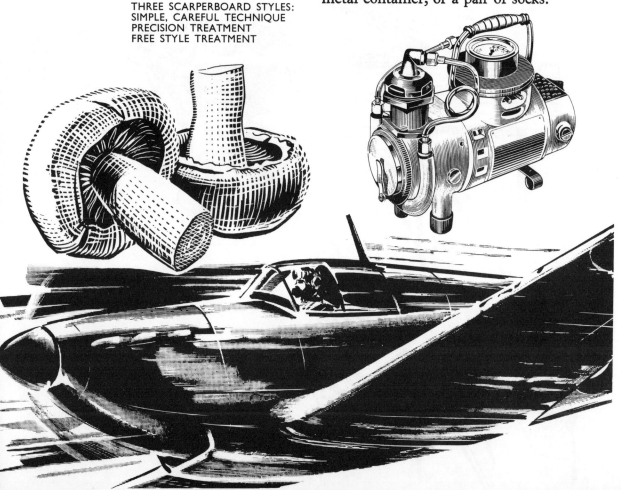

OTHER TECHNIQUES IN LINE

As we have already shown, there are many techniques. There is also always scope for new and experimental treatments. Only a few styles can be shown here. Study the line illustrations in books, newspapers and magazines to discover the diversity of techniques in use. Then only constant practice will enable you to become proficient in one or more techniques.

FREE STYLE BRUSH TREATMENT

PEN TREATMENT USING A
'NOT' SURFACED BOARD

FASHION DRAWING

In this branch of commercial art, too, techniques are varied, in line, in wash, and often in a combination of the two. Newspapers and women's magazines must be studied for drawing techniques, demand more thought than simply drawing correctly in detail. Elegance, grace, an exaggerated dignity in the figure, even hauteur, may all be used by the artist as a means of expressing the right atmo-

WASH   WASH AND LINE   LINE

but the Fashion Artist must also study clothes and how they are made and worn.

Study the work of fashion artists very carefully. Note the exaggeration which is employed, not only in the figure, such as in the extra length of the legs, but also in the pose, the features, and in the style which the garment is meant to express. The atmosphere to be conveyed by a particular fashion drawing can sphere in an illustration for 'high fashion' or expensive clothes. On the other hand, a drawing for youthful or inexpensive clothes may require an atmosphere of vivacity and simple charm.

Fashion drawing is a specialized part of commercial art. You must study fashion drawing in itself, and you must continually study clothes, hair-styles, make-up and so forth.

TECHNICAL ILLUSTRATION

Technical illustration requires the artist to be at least part draughtsman. Before you start on this subject you must have a sound grasp of the perspective section on pages 16 to 34.

Your equipment should include hot pressed or Bristol board, cartridge and tracing paper, Indian ink, pen and pencil compasses, ruling pen, 45° and 60° transparent set squares, pen with fine nib, pair of dividers, French curves, fine and large brushes (say Nos. 1 and 5), fairly hard pencils, process white paint, a hard rubber and a soft gum eraser.

Technical illustration covers a wide field—trade journals, engineering books, maintenance manuals and so forth. The object is clarity, a technical illustration that will be easily understood by the layman. The technique mostly used is line. This gives a more clearly defined illustration and reproduces well and cheaply on most types of paper.

Aeronautical, motoring and similar journals show the variety in technical illustration and the degree of skill and exactness that is required.

We remind you again that perspective is the foundation of this work, giving depth and reality to your drawing. You will also use perspective to convey size, especially when drawing a long object. Establish your axis and axle at right angles to each other, determining the length of both, before drawing ellipses.

Another important item is shading technique. If you have the object before you it should be placed with the light coming from a definite direction; if you are drawing from a photograph you should imagine the light direction. A study of technical illustrations will show you how different shading techniques are used according to the nature of the material and to throw certain parts into high relief. Lines, dot stipple, adhesive transparent tints laid on the drawing, mechanical tints added by the blockmaker and solid blacks all play a part. Scraperboard is also used, of course.

Your first sketch can be on bank or cartridge paper to get your proportions correct and the main details in position.

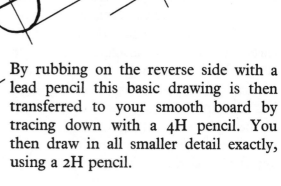

By rubbing on the reverse side with a lead pencil this basic drawing is then transferred to your smooth board by tracing down with a 4H pencil. You then draw in all smaller detail exactly, using a 2H pencil.

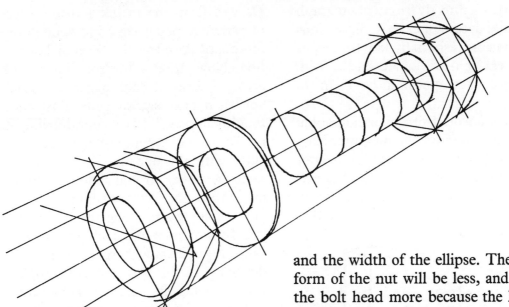

and the width of the ellipse. The ellipse form of the nut will be less, and that of the bolt head more because the latter is farther away and has a more circular ellipse.

Now line in with your ruling pen, or if a freer style is desired, with an ordinary pen. Take great care with the threaded section of the bolt; notice the greater space between each thread at the centre of the bolt compared with the ends, to give roundness and perspective.

LAYING OUT THE JOB

We will begin with a simple nut, bolt and washer. Place them before you in the perspective that you intend to follow. Mark out the centre axle line of the bolt (see bottom of facing page).

Decide the amount of taper in the bolt perspective without a vanishing point as indicated above. Determine the diameter of the washer in perspective

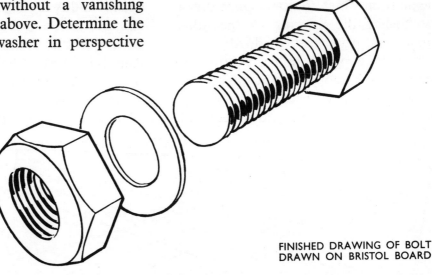

FINISHED DRAWING OF BOLT
DRAWN ON BRISTOL BOARD

PROPORTION IN TECHNICAL ILLUSTRATIONS

If you work directly from a photograph you should ascertain exactly the various measurements, especially lengthwise, as the camera can exaggerate and a 9-in. long object may appear to be 15 in. in length.

When you work from an orthographic drawing or blueprint the measurements are known, but an idea of the overall proportion pictorially can be obtained in the following way. Suppose that the subject, broadly sketched, occupies this shape.

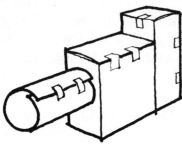

Cut the two sections out of stiff cartridge paper and make them up exactly to scale. Place them before you in the position and perspective that you require and you will have the basic shape from which to draw. Once this is established the drawing of the other component parts may be added.

Vanishing points in perspective are difficult to establish if the object has 'slow' perspective because a drawing-board many feet wide would be required.

Draw a firm line in ink across a sheet of cartridge paper covering your drawing-board. Use this line as your horizon line. Now draw a horizon line in ink across a sheet of bank paper, on which you then next sketch your illustration roughly in pencil. Place your drawing on the board so that its horizon line coincides with the one underneath on the cartridge paper. If you slide your drawing to the right your vanishing point can now be anywhere along the line to the left. By moving it to the left you can fix a vanishing point anywhere along the line to the right. In this way you can complete your drawing in accurate perspective.

Another aid is the double-grid shown below and used as a basis in the 'slow' perspective drawing on page 115. It is drawn in ink, for permanent use, and you sketch on bank paper placed over the grid. Several grids can be made, with varying perspective angles, and kept for use.

SECTIONED AND EXPLODED TECHNICAL ILLUSTRATIONS

Sectioned illustrations are often needed and the ability to visualize the appearance of parts inside the casing is required. Complete the outline drawing of the main body first. When sectioning, indicate the correct thickness of the metal or other material, taking into account the effect of any perspective.

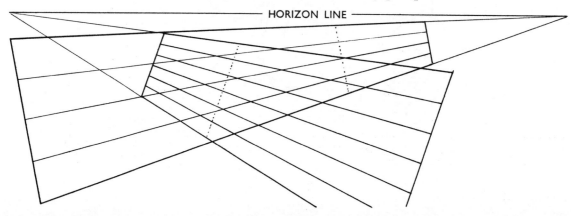

HORIZON LINE

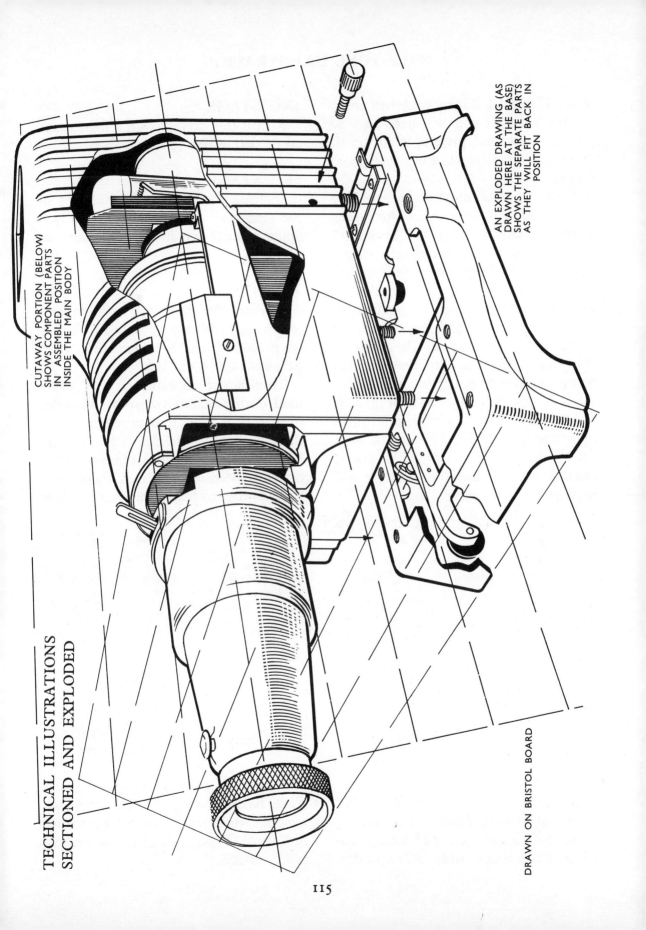

TECHNICAL ILLUSTRATIONS
SECTIONED AND EXPLODED

CUTAWAY PORTION (BELOW)
SHOWS COMPONENT PARTS
IN ASSEMBLED POSITION
INSIDE THE MAIN BODY

AN EXPLODED DRAWING (AS
DRAWN HERE AT THE BASE)
SHOWS THE SEPARATE PARTS
AS THEY WILL FIT BACK IN
POSITION

DRAWN ON BRISTOL BOARD

WASH DRAWING (known as half-tone)

The materials you will need include process black and process white paint, and rough cartridge paper or not surfaced boards.

Your technique must be governed by the fact that you are painting for reproduction. Your drawing will be photographed and a printing plate or block will be made from the negative. The image, therefore, must be crystal clear and, generally speaking, it should have plenty of contrast and power. If you make any alterations to the drawing they should not be discernible by normal scrutiny because the camera will reproduce all imperfections. Constant practice is necessary to acquire wash control for half-tone illustration. To grade a wash from light to dark within a given area is difficult at first and this exercise will help you.

2ND STAGE

Repeat this process with a lighter tint on the left. Allow to dry.

3RD STAGE

Increase the shadow on the right in the same way as in Stage 1. When dry, apply another overall tint, lightening to one side.

4TH STAGE

Increase the dark tone at right and soften edges quickly. A few deft touches of process white for highlights, then perhaps a touch of black.

Transparent adhesive tape is often used during the above process in order to keep clear edges to the drawing. Use the tape lightly, pressing only with the fingernail along the edge adjacent to the drawing to ensure that it is sealed. For curved edges, place the tape lightly

1ST STAGE

Work sideways on and brush quickly from end to end. Rinse brush quickly, shake out surplus water and soften both edges with a single stroke. Allow to dry.

across and trim to shape with a sharp blade before sealing the edge. Another material which can be used for masking is Varnish Paper, which has a slightly tacky surface.

PAINTED ON NOT FASHION BOARD

Imagine that the object is divided into four tones—dark, medium, light and white. This gives a three-dimensional appearance.

Where a light tone turns a corner to a dark tone an increase of dark at the turning point makes the object more realistic and diamatic. A certain amount of exaggeration is necessary because during the reproduction process some of the tone strength may be lost. Practise laying both graded and perfectly flat washes and always allow one wash to dry before applying another. Do not attempt to increase a wash strength after you have applied very dark detail as it will 'pick up'.

'Line and tone' is the term used to describe artwork which combines both line and half-tone, that is wash and ink lines or solids. The technical details of how this type of work is reproduced are given in the printing and blockmaking sections.

The commercial artist's reason for using this technique is to combine in one piece of artwork the maximum amount of contrast; it is effective when printed on good quality smooth paper and gives extra impact to illustrations on newsprint. Line and tone can be combined in figure work to give extra emphasis or contrast, or, say, a small and detailed part of an engineering illustration, to which it is desired to draw the reader's attention, can be depicted in line while the rest is drawn in wash.

As a general rule, the essence of a line and tone sketch is to make effective use of clear whites and solid blacks, while half-tone is used to hold the drawing together and to show texture. When you have completed your preliminary wash drawing, trace down and ink in all solids, and some outlines where these are required. Do not outline everything everywhere; the interest in this type of drawing is in its distribution of light and dark, with outline kept to a minimum except where contour or emphasis is necessary. Do not attempt painstaking modelling in detail everywhere; keep this only for the important parts of the drawing.

Where the wash ends in a 'vignetted' edge, without a deliberate contour line or edge, the reproduction process often results in a hard edge not intended by the artist. A sketch of this nature requires skilled handling of brush and pen and a sense of how much of your picture should be left to the imagination of the reader. You must restrain any desire to fill in parts of the drawing which are best left alone, yet suggest enough to hold the interest and attention of the reader.

THE AEROGRAPH AND PHOTO RETOUCHING

The aerograph is an instrument for blowing a fine spray of colour on to a drawing or photograph.

The paint is put into a receptacle in the instrument, which is connected by a flexible tube to a compressed air supply, and the strength of the spray is controlled by lever movement. The nearer the aerograph is held to the paper the more concentrated is the spray, and if it is held farther away the spray is diffused more and gives a lighter application of the colour. The aerograph, or airbrush, produces a smoother, more even area of tint than can be done by laying a wash with a brush. It is used for backgrounds, finely graded shading which can look almost photographic, delicate vignetted edges, and for subtle concentrations of light or dark tones without hard edges.

The aerograph is used for retouching photographs—for improving tone values to get a clearer reproduction, amending or spraying out certain parts and so forth. Masking is used, cut to shape, and placed around the part to be sprayed, when sharply defined edges are required.

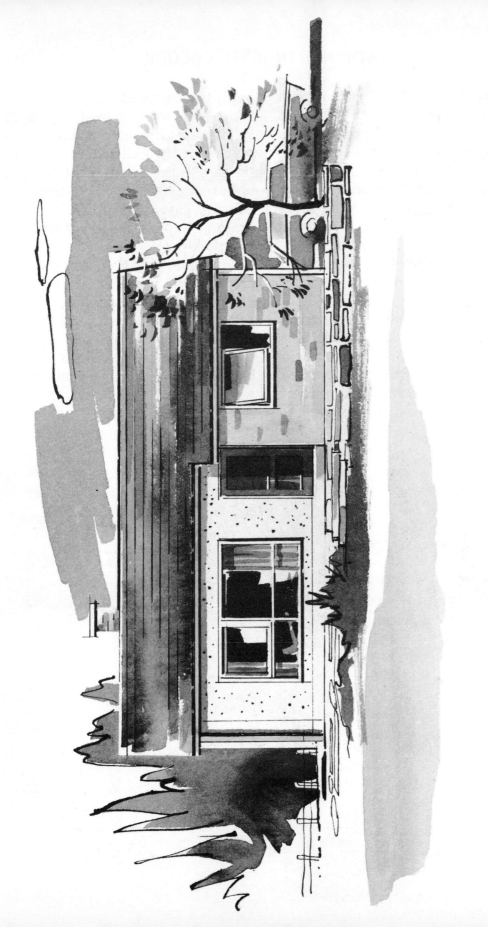

PAINTING IN BODY COLOUR

Body colour is black and white process paints mixed together to give a shade of grey. It is often used in 'wash' drawings designed for reproduction when firmer and less limpid-looking tone is required.

Broadly speaking, there are two ways of using this method; one is by a flat area of tone with no attempt to grade from light to dark, and the other is by painting with a more fluid mix and so working light and dark tones together while wet.

For technical reasons concerning photography, a series of special grey colours are made. They are graded in tone and ready for use, their purpose being to ensure an exact reproduction of the various tones in a drawing when it is being photographed.

Start by working in flat areas. You will find that it is difficult at first to paint an awkward shaped area in grey and at the same time to keep it flat and evenly opaque (this is one of the uses of the airbrush, page 118). Do not overfill your brush with colour and do not try to work too quickly.

If you mix your own body colour, use process white with lamp or ivory black. On this page are examples of flat tints painted in body colour, grading from light to dark while wet, and shading in body colour in clearly defined tones with highlights painted in with pure process white.

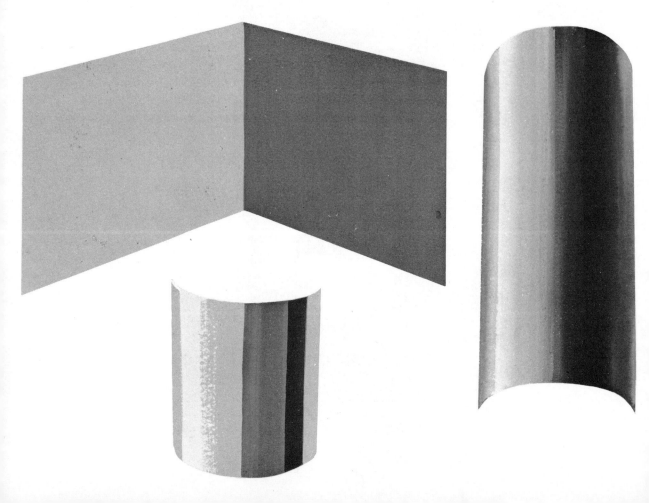

BODY COLOUR: FLAT TONE BACKGROUND
WITH MODELLING ON FIGURE

BODY COLOUR: FLAT TONES WITH INK OUTLINES

MAGAZINE ILLUSTRATION

There is considerable scope for the commercial artist in book and magazine illustration. In books the demand for illustration is mainly in the juvenile field, and in educational, technical and similar books. An accurate knowledge of the subject and skill in one or more techniques of drawing are needed.

Magazines come and go, and change, but always there are a large number of them and between them they cater for every type of reader interest. A study of even a few of the widely different magazines that are published weekly or monthly will show the immense variety of magazine illustration that is used. The artist who wishes to illustrate magazine stories and articles should study the publications in which he feels that there could be opportunities for his particular talents and interests.

We will not deal here directly with designs and drawings that are used in magazines to illustrate articles and other special features. A knowledge of these requirements can be gained by studying the necessary journals. Here we will concern ourselves with weekly and monthly magazines which publish fictional and biographical stories in black and white, two colours, or full-colour.

The following pages will give you a general idea of how the artist is briefed for this kind of work, and how to plan the type of illustration that is required. Every commercial artist is continually adding to his reference file and good magazine illustrations should be kept and filed in the same way.

Each magazine has its own style of appearance. That is to say, if you are at all familiar with the publication the most casual glance at it should be sufficient for you to recognize it by name. The layout of the pages each follow broadly the particular style of that magazine and the illustrations that go with the stories are an integral part of that style.

How does the artist start?

The magazine's Art Editor must be aware of the type of work of which the artist is capable and has decided that this is fitting to the subject of the story. The position on the page and the area which the illustration will occupy are decided, and the artist is briefed regarding the views of the Art Editor, who must also consider this particular illustration in its relation to other stories and articles in that issue of the magazine. The artist will have a copy of the manuscript to read and study.

Suppose that the story is dramatic and that the setting is a harbour. Many things must be considered if the sketch is to be authentic and have a natural atmosphere. What are the characters in the story wearing? If the story is an historical one, for example, what was the fashion in that period? What should be the facial characteristics of the people? What kind of horse and cart might be seen? What type of ships in the harbour? Were there any street lamp posts at that period? You will study the manuscript for information on these and similar points and if necessary do some research of your own. Are colours mentioned in the story? Is any particular time of the day indicated? All the details in your illustration must be correct.

The artist is likely to be given an incident or scene to portray that will add colour and flavour to the story without anticipating a climax that would steal the author's thunder. The artist is helping from behind the scene, not in front giving the game away!

The artist reads the story, perhaps several times. A rough layout is now prepared, actual size, and on it is marked the position and shape to be taken by the text. Unless it has been decided that the illustration will be 'bled off' the rough sketch does not exceed the column widths or the depths indicated by the Art Editor. An illustration is said to 'bleed', or be 'bled off', if it extends beyond the normal type area of the page into the margins and off the edge of the paper.

The artist now has a free hand in portraying the scene. The 'rough' that he presents must be clear to the Art Editor. A pencil sketch does not convey enough detail; a single colour sketch in wash or body colour is indicated if the reproduction is to be half-tone, or a two-colour sketch in the actual colours to be used if a second colour is employed in the printing. In the case of a full-colour illustration a lot must be done, even at the 'rough' stage, as the Art Editor will wish to see that the colours are correct as well as satisfying himself about other details. It can take as long or longer to prepare a satisfactory 'rough' as to do the finished artwork. Where a title illustration is required the artist will most probably not be expected to do the lettering that may cross over it; he will be told by the Art Editor where this will be placed so that it does not conflict with any part of the artist's drawing.

On page 125 is an imaginary layout of a magazine page. It is intended to show some of the more obvious pitfalls to avoid and the necessity of keeping the composition well-balanced on the page, bearing in mind the size and shape of the magazine and the appearance of the type surrounding or near to the illustration. Examine the layout carefully before you read further, then see how your criticisms compare with the following.

The most glaring fault is the title lettering positioned across the face. The main figure is badly posed and too central on the page, and it is 'stepped' awkwardly and too close to the type matter. There is not enough shown of the figure on the left, the head is severed from the body, and the hands of this and the central figure distract by their nearness to each other. Finally, there is too much space left blank near the bottom.

This section can be no more than a brief introduction to the subject of magazine illustration; the rest is up to you. Sound basic drawing ability, especially in figure work, is essential.

Style and technique are then needed to give your illustrations an individual quality; originality is always an asset, but remember that only the best is good enough for magazine illustration, so that you must develop the basic quality of your drawing, master the conventional techniques, before you start to experiment. Practice and observation must never stop. And you can be encouraged by the fact that magazine Art Editors are invariably interested in a new artist's work, provided that it reaches the standard that is being published today.

Other pages in this Commercial Art section mention the fact that finished artwork for reproduction is generally prepared larger than the actual size that it is published. An easy way to enlarge a magazine illustration 'rough' (unless you have an enlarged photostat copy made from which you can make a tracing) is by the squares method which is illustrated below.

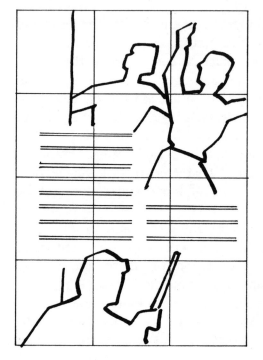

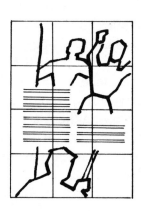

Some students find that lettering has a fascination for them that exceeds their interest in general drawing and painting. There is a wide range of type faces available today for all general purposes, but there is a constant need for hand-drawn lettering because it is an integral part of the complete design of an advertisement, poster, showcard, book jacket or pack. Good lettering is an art. Here we are concerned with its commercial use.

The Roman alphabet is the foundation of our lettering and the student should first study thoroughly the Roman based style and the characteristics of each individual letter. New type faces are constantly being designed. On these pages are three Roman based alphabets—two were designed in the nineteen-thirties, Perpetua by Eric Gill, Times by Stanley Morison, and the third is Caslon, which was designed by William Caslon in the seventeen-thirties. Study these letters until you can draw them accurately from memory; pages 128–129 show you how to set about this. There are, of course, many other Roman based styles.

PERPETUA TITLING

ABCDEFGHIJKLMNOPQRS
TUVWXYZ? 1234567890

TIMES ROMAN

abcdefghijklmnopqr
stuvwxyz
ABCDEFGHIJKL
MNOPQRSTUVW
XYZ? 1234567890

ABCDEFGHIJKLM
NOPQRSTUVWXYZ

abcdefghijklmnopqrstuvwxy

You next learn the Sans Serif style of letter; Sans Serif means 'without serifs'. As with the Roman style, with its many variations in which sometimes the original classic proportions are departed from almost completely, there are numerous versions of the Sans Serif letter. They may be condensed or extended, light or bold, according to the particular need. A good model to start from is the Gill Sans type face, designed by Eric Gill in 1929.

ABCDEFGHIJKLM
NOPQRSTUVW
XYZ? abcdefghij
klmnopqrstuvwxyz
BOLD LIGHT **ETC**

THE LAYOUT OF LETTERING

Practise your lettering in a size that is large enough to enable you to judge your spacing accurately and to produce a fine finish. You will need all the normal equipment mentioned on other pages, with the emphasis on a range of Gillot nibs, sandpaper block to keep your pencil sharp, Nos. 1 and 2 sable hair brushes for fine finishing and larger sizes for stylized brush work lettering. Keep your brushes, nibs, ruling pen and ink compasses clean; a clumsily inked line can ruin a well-drawn letter.

diagonals should be very slightly less than the vertical thicknesses; this is not necessary in lighter versions. The thin lines do not vary in this way.

Letters which curve at the top or

WEIGHT AND SPACING

Correct weight, size and spacing is the key to good lettering. Each letter is formed differently and occupies a differently shaped area compared with its neighbour, but all must appear to be of the same weight and have the same space between. Here are some guiding rules.

To ensure an optically even appearance in weight, curved strokes should be slightly thicker at the middle than the vertical strokes. In heavy styles the

bottom should come outside the lines. The same rule holds for slanted serifs.

Well-designed letters can be spoilt by bad spacing. Here is an example.

FILTER

The spacing between letters varies and does not remain constant as above. Now look at the following.

FILTER

The 'L' is tucked under the arm of the 'T'. The 'I' is farther away from the vertical stroke of the 'L' which comes next to it. The spacing between each of the letters looks the same. Good spacing is a matter of judgment and practice. The widest space is where the vertical of one letter is next to the vertical of another letter; this space becomes less according to the nature of the letters adjoining.

T×RAI×N

In the word above the spaces marked with an X each occupy approximately the same area of space; the completed word looks right and is easy to read.

Italic letters developed out of the cursive scripts of the sixteenth century and are used to give emphasis to a word or phrase, for sub-headings, and the narrow form employed is useful where space is restricted. The Caslon italics are still a good model of this form and should be studied in their larger sizes.

The basis of good lettering, then, is a study of the foundation styles, Roman and Sans Serif, and an understanding of how to achieve correct spacing, weight and an even size. Then you can proceed to infinite experiment in styles.

Willow

ADVERTISING

CAPTIONS

for exhibitions

package DESIGNING

MACHINERY

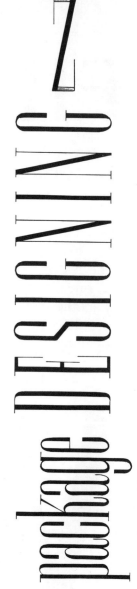

and display

ROMAN *Serifed Letter*	Ro	Ro	Ro	R
	OLD STYLE	MODERN	GROTESQUE	GROT. EXPANDED
EGYPTIAN *or slab serif*	E	E	E	E
	NORMAL	CONDENSED	EXPANDED	GROTESQUE
'SANS' 'no' serifs	S	S	S	S
	NORMAL	CONDENSED	EXPANDED	GROTESQUE

SCRIPT — SCRIPT STYLES IN PEN...

Formal and Informal Script

A ball-end pen gives an even weight letter

...WITH A BRUSH

Gets Attention!

LAYOUT

What is a layout? It is most often the design for an advertisement. Or it may be the design for a folder, catalogue, magazine page or almost any piece of printed matter. The person who does this work is a layout artist but there are variations within this definition.

The layout man, or woman, is usually employed in an Advertising Agency. Our concern is the principles of layout itself but you will understand these more easily if you have a general idea of the layout man's place in things.

Layout is skilled, creative, always interesting and often exciting work. It requires a wider knowledge of its many related subjects than does any other department of commercial or advertising art. We will explain this very briefly.

The purpose of an advertisement is to sell either a product or a service. The layout man's task is to design the advertisement so that it will do this effectively; the skilled and intelligent layout man will be able to work with the minimum of guidance but always, in a greater or lesser degree, he will need assistance from others, specialists in related subjects.

The modern Advertising Agency is an organization which plans, creates and places advertising for its clients, to sell their goods or services. It employs men and women who are trained in market and consumer research so that they can assess sales possibilities and customer requirements for a product; media men who study where the advertising should be placed to reach the right people; and copywriters, layout men, artists, lettering artists, typographers, production men who are concerned with printing and blockmaking, and others. One advertisement can cost anything up to around £5,000 or more, which would be the cost of a full-page in a newspaper with a top circulation, so that its design cannot be undertaken without serious study.

To whom is the advertisement to be addressed—men or women, or both? To which age group? To a sophisticated audience or otherwise? What are the product's best-selling features? What kind of paper is the advertisement to be printed on? The layout man takes careful note of these and other facts which may be supplied to him. Now to design the layout.

How do we start? There can be no set rules; remembering that the object of the advertisement is to SELL something, the degree of control that the layout man has over his work depends on the extent of his ability in this direction and the degree of all-round technical skill he has developed. The copywriter may initiate the layout by providing the headline and copy, and he in turn may have been guided in these by information supplied by the research team. How the layout is developed depends therefore on particular circumstances, but the more all-round ability and advertising intelligence that the layout man has, the more completely will he control the design of the layout. A top layout man is given plenty of freedom, another may elaborate from a rough visual prepared by a visualizer or develop his layout from material given to him by a copywriter. Your position in the ranks of layout men rests on how truly creative you are in all the factors which contribute to layout design, and on how knowledgeable you are in the mechanical processes by which it is reproduced and which therefore affect its design.

VARIATIONS IN IDEAS

Here are two of the many ways in which a subject could be presented. A layout is a visual idea, composed from words and illustration with both of these directed to one end—to sell the product. A humorous approach (see top right) can be very effective, but humour in layout must sell as well as amuse.

LAYOUT MATERIALS

Almost all art materials are useful to the layout man; soft lead pencils, carbons, soft pastels and a comprehensive range of designer's colours, lamp black, process white, coloured inks and dyes, masking fluid, adhesive lettering and tints, pens, brushes—there is a great variety of equipment in use today.

TECHNIQUE AND METHOD

A layout is drawn to look as it will appear when it is printed. Some artists have a talent for ideas, or for developing other people's ideas, a sound sense of commercial design and the experience and ability to indicate good lettering and type styles quickly and accurately. A good layout artist can emulate known artists' techniques and styles, and pursue new ones. He knows reproduction methods. His layouts are crisp, clean, presenting positive ideas in an attractive way.

Generally, layouts are prepared on layout paper, or on heavy white paper such as Kent. Layouts on bank paper are done in pencil, or ink and pastel, in a fairly free treatment. Black and grey pastel give a nice half-tone effect, the illustration being first drawn lightly in black ink with a pen or brush. A small piece of layout paper can be used to keep the edges sharp when using pastel. The

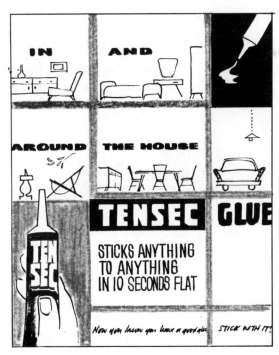

layout is then mounted on white cartridge paper.

A brochure would be carefully laid out on paper from a preliminary rough visual of the various page layouts.

The same basic copy has been used here in each layout, but the emphasis has been altered in each arrangement to show different ways of presenting what are virtually the same contents. Composition should be simple but seldom symmetrical; avoid duplication of the same widths and depths.

FOLDERS AND BROCHURES

A simple formula for a two-colour folder shows the use of a second colour (grey) in panel shapes, with extra heavy black rules for emphasis. Illustrations could be photographs, or sketches drawn in an interesting technique. A folder layout is usually prepared on fairly heavy white paper, in poster colour and black ink. Rough lettering on layouts looks neater if lightly drawn but quite definite rules, to give an edge to the top and base of the letters, are retained on the paper. A layout artist should know standard printing paper sizes, to ensure that his layouts are practical and economic in their size and shape. Familiarity with type face styles and appreciation of their different uses, and ability to calculate

the amount of space required for text, is essential; page 138 introduces you to typography.

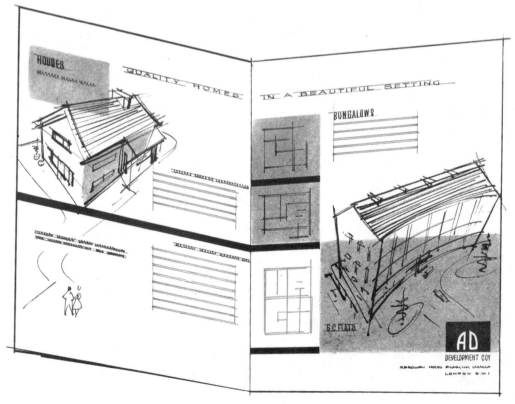

The printer's layout indicates to the compositor how the layout is to be displayed. You should know what type faces and sizes your printer has before giving your instructions. Body matter, or text, is supplied typed on a separate sheet and keyed with a reference letter to its place in the layout.

TYPOGRAPHY

Lettering is an important part of commercial art, as described on pages 126 to 131, and some artists specialize in it exclusively. Until printing with movable type was discovered all books were written by hand in capital letters known as uncials and based on the Roman alphabet of capitals, which is the basis of all Western alphabets except that of Russia which is based on Greek letters. Cursive writing then gradually evolved, by skilful use of quill pen and reed, in many different and beautiful forms. Movable type was first used in Europe in the first half of the fifteenth century. Finally, metal type was produced and a standard system of manufacture adopted. In a printer's composing room the metal type letters are kept in partitioned trays, or cases. Capitals are known as 'upper case' letters, small characters as 'lower case' letters because capitals were once kept in an 'upper case' and small letters in a 'lower' one.

Typography is the art and operation of printing from type. The type character shown on the facing page will help you to understand this brief description of the typographic process.

MEASUREMENT

This is based on the 'point' system, 12 points to one em, 6 ems or 72 points to an inch. Types may be cast in sizes as small as 5-point or as large as 144-point. The point size refers to the body of the type, shown in the illustration opposite. You will see that space is provided between lines of type by the shoulders which are necessary for the few characters which have ascenders or descenders. Nine lines of 8-point type set solid, for instance, will occupy an inch in depth. Or it may be 'leaded' to give more space between the lines. Leads are strips of metal slightly less than type high and these are also in point sizes. This column of type, for instance, is set in 12-point Plantin, with 2-point leading, 17 ems wide. For spacing words, and sometimes letters, so that the line will set to its correct length, spaces and quads are used.

The em is variable as a unit of area according to its point size; its name derives from the fact that it was based on the width of the capital M. In the same way an 'en' space is half an em. It is the 12-point em which is used as a standard for measuring the depth and width of a page or type area. A type area of, say, 4 by $3\frac{2}{3}$ in. would be 24 by 22 ems, the ems being meant as 12-point ems. All type matter is of one standardized height, $\frac{11}{12}$ of an inch, or to be exact, 0.918 in.

A layout designer should possess a printer's rule, a 12-in. rule which is also divided into printer's measurements. An approximate method for estimating the amount of space required for text is to count the number of characters, in a type specimen book, in a given length and in a particular point size. This column of type, for instance, sets approximately 37 characters, 12-point size, in a line of 17 ems wide. The depth required can be easily calculated from the number of lines of type, more if leading—such as 1-point, 2-point leading—is used between the lines. Care must be taken to avoid type being set in lines which are too long for the point size so that they become difficult to read. For instance, 8-point type should not be set less than 8 ems, or more than 14 ems wide, while a line of 12-point type should be set to not less than 14 or more than 24 ems.

The only satisfactory way to estimate the space required for display setting and headings in large type is to trace or measure the characters in the point size and face to be used.

COMPOSITION

Type can be set either by hand or machine. In hand setting the compositor selects the drawers, or cases, containing the size and face of type he wishes to use. He then removes individual letters and arranges them in a 'composing stick' which he holds in his left hand, transferring the composed type at intervals to a galley, a form of metal tray. The type is then proofed from the galley, and these are called galley proofs, for corrections to be made. Type and blocks, if any, are then arranged together on the composing frame, proofed, corrected, then taken to the 'imposing stone', which is a table with a perfectly level surface of iron. Here, the type and blocks are locked tight together in an iron frame known as a 'chase'. Before the chase or 'forme' is finally 'locked up' a block of wood with a perfectly level surface is placed on top of the type matter and tapped lightly with a mallet to ensure that everything in the chase is exactly 'type high'. The chase or forme is then ready for printing.

In machine setting, the operator sits before a keyboard similar to that of a typewriter. If it is a Linotype machine each line of type is produced in one piece of metal; a Monotype machine casts each letter separately. Machine setting is obviously very much faster than hand setting and the composed type is finally transferred to the printing forme.

The commercial artist and layout designer needs to have a knowledge of typographical processes and be familiar with various type face designs, so that his work is not only more complete, but also technically sound when it passes to those who have to reproduce it.

SOME TYPESETTING STYLES

This is 8pt Grotesque Bold Condensed, a forceful and business-like face, set solid

Here is 8pt Rockwell Light, set solid, an Egyptian slab-serif style letter

This is Rockwell Heavy, which would read more easily if the lines were leaded instead of set solid as here

Here is 8pt. Bodoni a modern type face which sets more letters to the line than Rockwell

6pt Bembo is very legible in this small size and is designed more in the traditional old style

These two lines are set in 6pt Times Roman and you will notice that they appear darker than the Bembo

6pt Gill Sans Medium sets slightly more characters to the length of line than does Times Roman as you can see here

These lines are set in 12pt Gill Sans Medium and leaded 2pt so that you can compare the effect with the columns of this book which are set 12pt Plantin and leaded 2pt in the same way as here

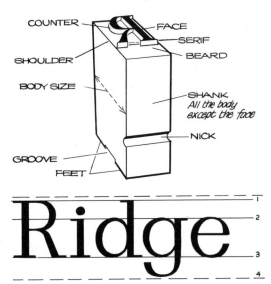

1. Ascender line. 2–3. The distance between these two lines is the 'X' height of the letter; this varies within the same point size according to the design of the type face. 4. Descender line.

The basic methods of printing are discussed on pages 143–144 and of these the most commonly used is letterpress. Blocks are used in letterpress printing to reproduce illustrations and hand-drawn lettering. An artist should have a knowledge of blockmaking, or process engraving, if he wishes to produce work that will reproduce well.

Just as were the first individual type letters cut from wood, so the first printing of pictures was from woodcuts, the artist tooling away the unwanted parts to leave the design in relief. The process block prints basically in this way; the image is transferred to a metal plate photographically and the unwanted parts are etched to below surface level so that the design is left in relief.

There are two main kinds of blocks, line and half-tone, with variations of each.

LINE BLOCKS

These are used for printing artwork which is executed in line, using solid blacks (or solid colours) and clear whites and involving various line techniques, some of which have been described on previous pages, such as simple line, dot stipple, dry brush, mechanical tints and so forth.

The drawing is photographed, and a negative is prepared to the required size, using a special kind of film. This is then developed in a dark room and dried. The whites of the original image appear dark on the negative, the blacks clear. Now the negative is printed on to a sheet of polished zinc, the surface of which has first been coated with a substance which is sensitive to light. The plate is developed by washing away the unex-posed areas with water, the exposed parts having become hard and resistant to water. Heating is now used to make this hard enamel coating acid-resistant; the back is also protected from acid. The zinc plate is now put into an etching machine and the unprotected parts are etched away with nitric acid, leaving in relief the image required for printing.

The etching is done with care, the plate being taken from and returned to the acid bath several times, being well brushed each time with a red powder which engravers call 'dragon's blood' so that the acid does not weaken the sides of the exposed parts. After cleaning, any large unwanted areas of the plate are mechanically etched, or routed, proofs are taken from the plate, then it is mounted on wood to become 'type high', the same height as type. A line block is frequently called a 'zinco' because it is most commonly made from zinc.

COLOUR LINE BLOCKS

The process of making line blocks for printing in two or more colours is dependent on the way in which the artist prepares his drawing. The metal plates are made in the manner which has been explained, but a separate plate must be made for each colour and for this the colours in the original drawing must first be separated, photographically or by hand on the negative. A third way is for the artist to avoid the need for colour separation by the blockmaker, by this means often saving considerable expense and trouble during the reproduction process. There are several ways in which the drawing might be prepared to achieve this saving.

If the design is not too intricate the

main colour can be drawn in black on white board. A sheet of transparent Kodatrace is fixed temporarily on top of this and on it the second colour is carefully drawn, also in black. If more colours are involved, the operation is repeated for each colour. The separate drawings must fit together accurately and, as a general rule, a colour should overlap its neighbour by a fraction— one sixty-fourth of an inch is enough —to allow for slight variations during the printing.

Another method is for the artist to prepare a 'key' drawing. Here, the main colour is in black and the others are outlined only, also in black. With the original rough design in colour to guide him the blockmaker can prepare separate plates from this negative.

Even when the drawing is prepared in colour, it is often advisable that the drawing should not be executed in the colours to be used in the printing. Certain colour combinations can make the task of colour separation by the blockmaker very difficult. If an artist has to prepare a colour line drawing for reproduction, until he is thoroughly familiar with reproduction processes he should seek guidance before proceeding with the finished drawing. In an Advertising Agency or Commercial Studio the production staff can advise him how to prepare the drawing, and students might care to note that even artists who are experienced in drawing for reproduction often ask the blockmaker for his advice before preparing some drawings of this nature.

MECHANICAL TINTS

Page 107 explained how mechanical tints can be laid on the drawing by the artist. Tints are also applied by the blockmaker, either to the negative or direct to the plate before etching is done. Blockmakers issue tint cards or folders showing their tint range and they are similar to the artist tints illustrated on page 107, but of course there is a great variety of styles.

The parts of the drawing where the blockmaker is to apply tints is usually covered with a pale blue wash, or shaded with a blue pencil, and the tint number is indicated on the overlay. More than one tint can be used on a drawing and if the tint laying is intricate it is usual to outline these areas with thin ink lines. If these lines are to be removed after the tints have been applied, the blockmaker can be instructed to do this and, if the instructions are quite clear, it is not essential that the tint areas should be shaded in blue if the tint numbers are indicated.

HALF-TONE BLOCKS

Half-tone blocks are used when the illustration which is to be reproduced is either a wash drawing or a photograph. Drawings in body colour (see page 120), paintings in water-colours or oils, soft pencil drawings and certain other types of illustrations, are also reproduced by this method.

Half-tone blocks are made in approximately the same way as are line blocks. The most important difference is that all half-tone subjects are photographed through a screen. This is placed inside the camera, in front of the sensitized plate, and it is in effect a glass mesh formed by two sets of black parallel lines which cross each other at right-angles. The light can only pass through the squares and in this way the image is photographed on to the negative as a multitude of small dots of varying sizes. These can be seen if you look through a magnifying glass at a newspaper picture. The remaining procedure resembles that for a line block except that the metal may be either copper or zinc. The means by which the printing surface of the metal is made acid-resistant before the plate is etched may differ a little but the principle remains the same.

The plate then goes into an etching machine for its first etching. Copper is etched electrically or with iron perchloride; zinc is etched with nitric acid. Next, the dark portions of the picture are carefully painted over with acid-proof varnish and the plate is etched again so that the dots in the lighter areas of the picture become smaller. In this way the light and dark tone values of the picture are suitably reproduced. This operation may be repeated several times, skilled painting-out and careful etching being required to produce the correct tone values.

There is a range of screen sizes, or 'densities'. The size is determined by the number of parallel lines per inch on the screen, and these range between 45 and 225. The number of rulings to the inch determines the size of the dots on the negative and the screen size to be used is governed by the kind of paper on which the block is to be printed. The screen sizes most commonly used are 55, 65, 85, 100, 120 and 133. Screens finer than 150 are seldom used. For newspapers the screen is generally either 55 or 65; for printing on art paper such as is used in the 'glossy' magazines, so called because the paper has a smooth and glossy surface, the screen would probably be 120. Coarse screen half-tone blocks, up to 85, are made of zinc, finer screen blocks of copper.

COMBINATION LINE AND HALF-TONE BLOCKS

This kind of drawing is dealt with on page 118. Briefly, both a line and a screen negative are made and skilfully combined, then etched together on one plate.

COLOUR HALF-TONE BLOCKS

It is not practicable to prepare a separate drawing for each colour, as can often be done for a line drawing which is in two or more colours, and the colours are separated photographically by the blockmaker.

The general process is the same as for monochrome half-tone blocks, except that a separate block is necessary for each colour to be printed. The drawing may be photographed two, three or four times, each time through a filter which extracts one colour only from the image. In this way a negative is obtained for each colour, printed on to a copper plate and etched.

A full colour range can be produced from the three primaries of red, yellow and blue; in printing, the yellow block is printed first, the red is printed on top, and finally the blue. Three-colour half-tone blocks such as these give an approximate full colour reproduction of the original, but if a richer black is required than is obtainable by a combination of the three primaries, a fourth 'black' block is used. A half-tone drawing in two or three colours is reproduced by two-colour half-tone, provided that the third colour results from the two primaries being used—a design in blue, red and purple, say, can be produced by superimposing a blue over a red plate, but a design in blue, red and green will require three blocks and printings.

Skill and judgment are needed in the making of colour half-tone blocks, notably in the retouching and etching, and the blockmaker craftsman must have a good colour sense. The blocks are, of course, more expensive than simpler ones. The blockmaker supplies 'progressive' proofs with a set of colour blocks; the blocks are proofed individually in their respective colours, then one proof shows the red superimposed over the yellow, the next shows the blue printed over these, and if a separate black is used a final proof shows the black printed over the other three colours. An example of full colour half-tone, including progressive proofs, appears on pages 153–156.

STEREOTYPING

Stereos are inexpensive replicas of original type or blocks. A 'flong' of papier-mâché-like material is moulded from the original under great pressure, and into the resulting matrix molten metal is poured and an exact replica is made.

ELECTROTYPING

Stereos are cast in white metal, but electros have a copper surface; they are used for replicas of fine screen half-tone or fine line blocks. Wax was first used for making the mould; now plastic is being used, and replicas similar to the electro are also made in plastic.

SUMMARY

New techniques in blockmaking are constantly evolving, resulting especially from electronic advances; we have described the basic principles.

PRINTING

There are three methods of printing. The most common is the relief method, where the parts which are to be inked are higher than the rest of the surface; this is the basis of LETTERPRESS printing. The intaglio method reverses this principle, the design being printed from a metal plate on which the parts to be inked are etched below the surface. The ink is received into these sunken parts, the surface automatically cleaned, and printed on to the paper under pressure. PHOTOGRAVURE is the main intaglio method. Thirdly, planographic printing means printing from a surface which is flat. This is made possible by the antipathy between grease and water (ink is greasy). LITHOGRAPHY is the chief planographic method.

LETTERPRESS

Wood type and letters were used for this process when it developed in Europe during the fourteenth century; it was known to the Chinese before this period. Now, as we have seen, metal type and blocks are used and letterpress has remained the simplest and most versatile of the printing processes. It is used for newspapers, many periodicals and magazines, for all kinds of 'jobbing' work from single-page leaflets to coloured brochures, and for a good deal of book printing.

The pages on typography and block-making have made clear much of this process. Type and blocks are assembled in a forme, then placed on a printing machine where the surface is inked and the ink transferred from here to the paper by pressure.

Letterpress machines are divided into three main types—platen, cylinder flat-bed, and rotary. In a platen, more limited in its size of printing area, pressure is applied to the paper and forme by a flat steel slab. The forme may be either vertically or horizontally placed, according to the kind of platen machine. In cylinder flat-bed machines, the forme (or formes) is placed on the machine and moves to and fro beneath an ink roller and a cylinder. The roller inks the printing surface, after which the impression cylinder applies pressure as the paper passes between it and the forme. Rotary presses are used for high-speed printing, such as for newspapers and many magazines. The forme is not used in its original state; instead, a stereo is cast from the complete forme in a semi-circular shape and this is fitted to a cylinder. The paper passes between this and the impression cylinder. Some idea of the size, complexity and running speed of a giant rotary press may be estimated from the fact that one machine can print over ten thousand copies of a forty-page newspaper in an hour—a web of blank newsprint being fed into the machine at one end, completely printed and folded newspapers emerging at the other end.

PHOTOGRAVURE

Flat-bed photogravure is now little used; photogravure is generally understood to mean photogravure printing by the rotary method. It is used to print magazines and similar material at high speeds where 'long runs' are concerned; the high cost of preparing the printing surface makes it uneconomic for 'short runs'. Illustrations are excellently reproduced on mediocre paper by this process, and a photogravure magazine can be recognized by the 'soft' effect of the printing and the slightly serrated type letter edges. Mail-order catalogues, for instance, colourfully illustrated, are often printed by this process when they are required in large quantities.

In photogravure all the preparation work is done by the printer; type matter is set in the usual way and proofed, then these proofs with the photographs or drawings are reproduced photographically on to a copper cylinder through a fine mesh screen. The cylinder is etched, the ink floods in to the tiny cells which vary in depth, surplus ink is scraped from the surface, then pressure transfers the ink from the recesses to the paper.

LITHOGRAPHY

'Lithos' means stone. Lithographic surface printing was first used at the end of the eighteenth century; in modern lithographic machines zinc or aluminium plates are used, the surface treated to resemble the porous lithographic stone. And, of course, by the 'photolitho' process, type and pictures are transferred to the plate photographically, in the same way as photogravure has developed from hand engraving. Lithographic half-tone resembles letterpress in that the picture is split into dots of varying sizes. The printing plate is dampened by a water-roller, the water being repelled by the greasy (printing image) parts. Ink adheres to the printing image, but not to the damp areas. The printing is then transferred by pressure to the paper.

Lithography is used for posters and showcards, also for books and other items requiring 'long runs'.

SUMMARY

The printing processes above have been described only briefly. Of others, the screen printing method, often used for showcards and posters, should be studied by the commercial artist.

END

SAMPLE ILLUSTRATIONS WITH FULL-COLOUR SECTION

The student is reminded here that the first 144 pages of this book have been printed by lithography, the process described on page 144. The last 16 pages are printed by letterpress, the method explained on page 143. Note the different paper used for the two sections. The first section is printed on a cartridge type of paper, ideal for 'litho' printing. An art paper is used for this section so that, printing from metal blocks and type, a 'glossy' effect is obtained. The monochrome half-tone blocks have been made to 120 screen. The full-colour half-tone blocks are 133 screen. You can turn back to the block-making section, page 140, to refresh your memory on how the various kinds of blocks are made.

The illustrations show many different modern commercial art techniques.

Scraperboard. *Artist: E. Meirion Roberts*

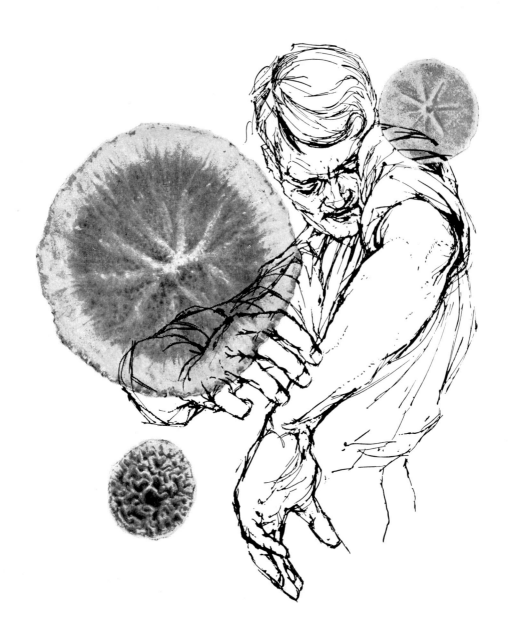

Above: Combined line and tone drawing.
Artist: J. N. Pill.
Studio: Mansfield Studio Ltd. Manchester.
Client: I.C.I. Pharmaceutical Division.

Facing: Combined line and tone drawing.
Artist: Gaby.
Advertising Agency: Millican Advertising
Limited, Liverpool.

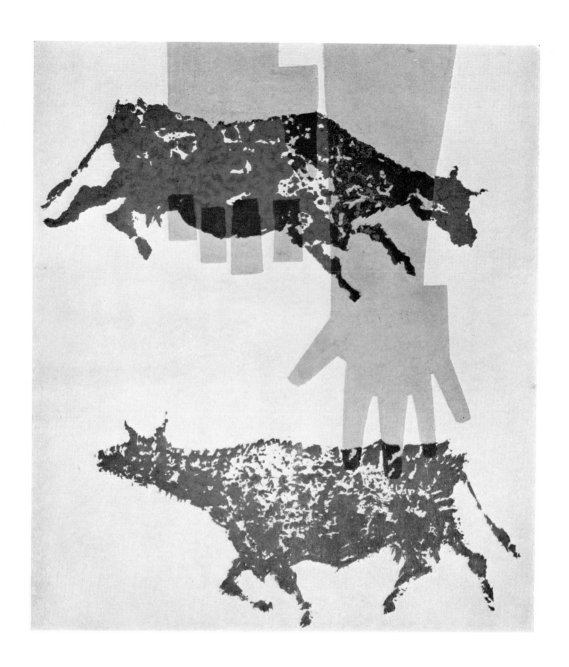

Above: Dry brush technique and flat tones, reproduced by half-tone block.
Artist: J. N. Pill.
Client: I.C.I. Pharmaceutical Division.

Facing: Brush technique, reproduced from an original in goauche colours.
Artist: J. N. Pill.
Studio: Mansfield Studio Ltd. Manchester.

Photographer : J. Allen Cash, F.I.B.P., F.R.P.S.
Client : Packaging Products Holding Group
Advertising Agency : Barnaby & Tarr Co. Ltd.

For the illustration below a black and white print was made by photographic processes from a normal photograph, top left, and a line block was made from the 'drop out' photographic print.

Pages 151-155. These pages show the progressive stages in four-colour half-tone printing.

Block of the yellow is printed first.

The red block printed over the yellow.

LOVELY TO LOOK AT ... DELIGHTFUL TO KNOW
Captivating
COLWYN BAY

The blue block is third to be printed.

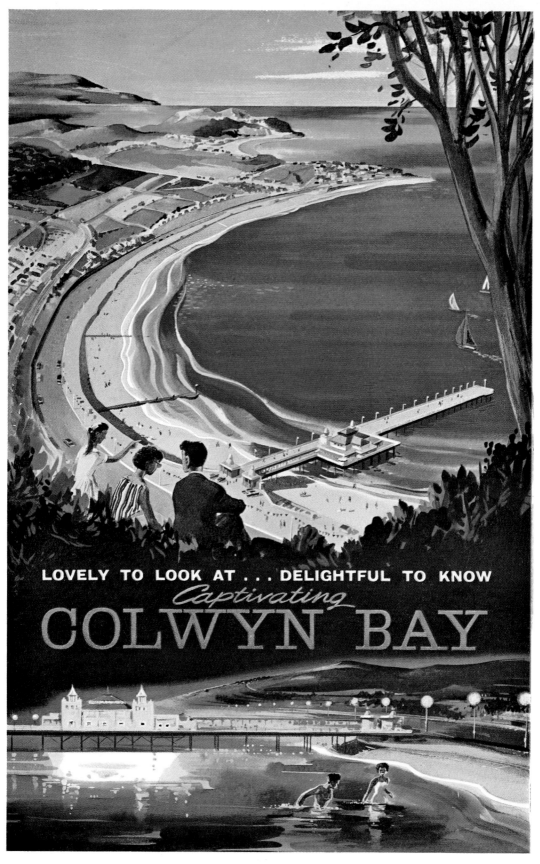

LOVELY TO LOOK AT ... DELIGHTFUL TO KNOW
Captivating
COLWYN BAY

Fourth printing is from the black block.

Three printings produce full-colour (page 153), fourth black printing adds to darker tones. Holiday Guide cover.

Design: Willington Advertising Limited, Colwyn Bay and Birmingham.
Client: Colwyn Bay Corporation.
Engravers: R. E. Jones & Bros. Ltd., Conway.

LOVELY TO LOOK AT . . . DELIGHTFUL TO KNOW
Captivating
COLWYN BAY

The black block as it looks by itself.

Left: A fine example of careful scraper-board work. Part only of the original drawing is reproduced here.
Artist: R. Moseley. Advertising Agency: Barnaby & Tarr Co. Ltd., Manchester.

Below: Another scraperboard drawing in a technique which contrasts with the facing drawing although the same medium is used.
Artist: E. Meirion Roberts.

Above and facing page: Examples of two reproductions from the same photograph. A squared-up half-tone block was first made from the photograph, used exactly as it was supplied by the photographer, and the result is shown above.

A cut-out half-tone block made from the same photograph as used for the block on the facing page, but after it had been retouched and background painted out. Both blocks reproduced by permission of *Quinton Hazell Ltd., Colwyn Bay.*

NORTH WALES

CROESO I GYMRU!
WELCOME TO WALES!

HOLIDAY   PLEASURE   TREVEL

This page: Delicate line drawing.
Artist : David I. Biddlecombe.
Client : British Railways.

LONDON
MIDLAND
REGION